T0319009

Cambridge Elements ☰

Public Economics
edited by
Robin Boadway
Queen's University

Frank A. Cowell
The London School of Economics and Political Science

Massimo Florio
University of Milan

THE ROLE OF THE CORPORATE TAX

Roger Gordon
University of California, San Diego

Sarada Sarada
University of Wisconsin System

CAMBRIDGE
UNIVERSITY PRESS

CAMBRIDGE
UNIVERSITY PRESS

University Printing House, Cambridge CB2 8BS, United Kingdom

One Liberty Plaza, 20th Floor, New York, NY 10006, USA

477 Williamstown Road, Port Melbourne, VIC 3207, Australia

314–321, 3rd Floor, Plot 3, Splendor Forum, Jasola District Centre,
New Delhi – 110025, India

79 Anson Road, #06–04/06, Singapore 079906

Cambridge University Press is part of the University of Cambridge.

It furthers the University's mission by disseminating knowledge in the pursuit of
education, learning, and research at the highest international levels of excellence.

www.cambridge.org
Information on this title: www.cambridge.org/9781108747998
DOI: 10.1017/9781108779982

© Roger Gordon and Sarada Sarada 2019

First published 2019

A catalogue record for this publication is available from the British Library.

ISBN 978-1-108-74799-8 Paperback
ISSN 2516-2276 (online)
ISSN 2516-2268 (print)

The Role of the Corporate Tax

Elements in Public Economics

DOI: 10.1017/9781108779982
First published online: August 2019

Roger Gordon
University of California, San Diego

Sarada Sarada
University of Wisconsin System

Author for correspondence: Roger Gordon, rogordon@ucsd.edu

Abstract: Existing corporate taxes distort many aspects of firm behavior. To the extent that the corporate tax rate is lower than personal tax rates, taxes favor corporate activity and favor retaining earnings rather than paying earnings out to employees and investors. Multinationals can avoid even these taxes by shifting income into tax havens. Given the ease with which multinationals can evade tax, the existing income tax structure faces major pressures, as reflected in average statutory corporate tax rates halving in recent decades. The Element speculates on alternative tax structures that will avoid these problems.

Keywords: corporate taxes, multinationals, optimal taxation, income shifting, tax evasion

ISBNs: 9781108747998 (PB), 9781108779982 (OC)
ISSNs: 2516-2276 (online), 2516-2268 (print)

Contents

1 Introduction

The aim of this Element is to provide an overview of the role of the corporate tax within a country's overall tax system. While there is a large existing literature on the optimal design of the personal income tax, guidelines for the choice of tax base and tax rate for the corporate tax have been remarkably limited.

A common feature of most of the past papers that do exist on this topic is the simplifying decision to examine the corporate tax in isolation from other taxes, except perhaps for a lump-sum tax. Another common simplification is the presumption that the corporate tax base is simply the normal return to capital invested in the corporate sector. The ensuing results concerning optimal corporate tax rates have been highly diverse and very different from the patterns seen in practice.

Probably the most cited paper in this past literature is Harberger (1962). Under the above assumptions and, in addition, assuming that the overall supply of capital is inelastic, Harberger (1962) analyzed the effects of a corporate tax on market allocations in a closed economy. There are clear efficiency costs from such a tax, artificially shifting capital from the corporate to the noncorporate sector. Under these conditions, the incidence of the tax seems to fall largely on existing capital. If the tax were the only alternative to a lump-sum tax, then there would be a potential role for the tax, trading off possible equity gains with these efficiency losses.

Harberger (1982) reexamines this conclusion in an open economy that is small relative to the world capital market. Here, the optimal tariff on imports of capital is zero on efficiency grounds. However, the tax again may create some equity gains due to the resulting fall in market wage rates, with government revenue coming more from high-skilled than from low-skilled workers, unlike with a lump-sum tax.

One challenge faced in this particular literature is that the observed pretax net (of depreciation) corporate profit rate (equal on average to around 10–12 percent per year) is much higher than what the stylized models above would forecast, given observed annual real interest rates of around 1–2 percent. The past literature has explored the implications of various explanations for this high observed corporate profit rate. Mintz (1996), for example, argues that this high corporate profit rate in part represents "rents" accruing to firms. If the amount of these rents is unresponsive to taxes, then the optimal tax rate would be 100 percent, raising revenue free of efficiency costs and arguably with equity gains, while avoiding distorting capital investments through the use of expensing.[1]

---

[1] Even if these rents are fixed ex post, anticipations of the future imposition of such a tax can change behavior (e.g. the amount of entrepreneurial activity), leading to a "time inconsistency" problem.

Another possible explanation for these excess profits is a risk premium, compensating investors for market risk when they invest in corporate equity. As long as firms are publicly traded, and equity markets function well, then Diamond (1967) argues that a tax on these profits, with revenue returned as a lump-sum to taxpayers,[2] would have no net effects on market allocations: The government (really citizens more broadly) simply becomes an implicit shareholder in the corporate sector. Investors then can readjust their direct purchases of equity to maintain an efficient allocation of risk across investors. Now, the corporate tax rate does not matter.

Domar and Musgrave (1944) also focus on the effects of a corporate tax when profits are high owing to a risk premium but assume some firms are not publicly traded, presumably due to lemons problems.[3] Now, the corporate tax serves to reallocate risk-bearing from the owners of a closely held firm to investors more broadly, creating an efficiency gain in the risk market.[4] The higher the corporate tax rate, the higher will be this efficiency gain, in principle arguing for a 100 percent tax rate.

It is striking that these past papers generate such extreme, and disparate, forecasts for the optimal corporate tax rate.[5] What is missing from this literature that helps explain the patterns of corporate tax structures used in practice?

The objective of this Element is to focus on a major omission from the above literature: interactions between the corporate income tax and the personal income tax. Individuals and firms have substantial discretion concerning whether their income is taxable under the corporate tax or under the personal tax, e.g. at a minimum a firm can choose to incorporate or to remain noncorporate.

In section 2, we summarize the past literature, looking at the effects of these combined tax provisions on corporate behavior, and find that distortions arise when there is any difference between the combined corporate and personal tax rate on corporate income compared to the personal tax rate on noncorporate income. For example, to the extent that the tax rate on corporate income is less than that on personal income, taxes discourage debt finance, encourage operating as a corporation, favor investment in the corporate sector, and favor compensation (in closely held firms) through shares in the firm rather than through wage payments.

---

[2] Other assumptions are that the tax allows expensing, to avoiding distorting investment, and full loss offset.

[3] Certainly, many firms are closely held.

[4] Investment incentives can again be maintained through the use of expensing.

[5] These papers are just a small sampling from the many papers examining the role of a free-standing corporate tax. See Mintz (1996) for further discussion.

Section 3 then examines the optimal corporate tax structure, starting with a focus on a closed economy setting in Section 3.2.[6] One traditional recommendation is a "partnership treatment" of corporate income. Under this treatment, shareholders include in their personal tax base their share of each corporation's income accruing that tax year, with no separate corporate tax. No country has attempted this, however. Partly, shareholders would be asked to pay tax on earnings they have not yet seen. More fundamentally, though, there are no data concerning a firm's earnings accrued between the dates of any given individual's purchase and sale of a share within the year other than the one calculation over the firm's fiscal year.

Instead, every country has imposed a separate tax on corporate income. To approximate production efficiency, as advocated based on the results in Diamond and Mirrlees (1971) and Saez (2002), the overall tax on any given source of income should be the same regardless of where this income accrued. This means that the sum of the corporate and personal taxes due on any given income source should approximate the personal taxes that would have been owed had this income instead accrued within a noncorporate firm and been taxable solely under the personal tax.

The discussion then turns, in section 3.3, to the added complications that arise in a global economy, where firms can easily shift their profits across countries, e.g. through transfer pricing, the location of borrowing, or the strategic location of patents. What tax provisions would be needed to implement production efficiency in an open economy, where such income-shifting opportunities exist? A direct extension of the findings for a closed economy shows that productive efficiency would be maintained when a country imposes a corporate tax on the profits accruing on any shares owned by domestic residents, regardless of the location of the firm or where these profits were earned. Existing regulations by the Organization for Economic Cooperation and Development (OECD), though, do not give a country the right to tax foreign-source income simply based on portfolio investments by domestic investors. For foreign direct investment (FDI), the regulations allow countries either to exempt foreign-source income of domestic multinationals from domestic corporate taxation (a territorial tax treatment) or to impose domestic corporate taxes on the foreign subsidiaries of domestic firms, with a credit for taxes paid abroad on this income (worldwide taxation).

Strikingly, we show in this section that the tax provisions under "worldwide" taxation are close to those suggested by the theory under a particular set of

---

[6] Here, we take the provisions of an optimal personal income tax as given, where optimal rates are presumed to be positive on labor income and perhaps on capital income as well, trading off equity gains with efficiency losses.

assumptions. One key assumption is that a country imposes no tax on the return to savings (including allowing expensing for all capital investments). One way to implement this zero tax on savings for cross-border investments by multinationals is to allow a deduction from corporate income when funds are shifted abroad[7] and then to tax all repatriated funds. This type of cash-flow tax at the border implies no distortion to investment decisions as long as tax rates are constant over time[8] but still imposes a comparable tax on any income shifted abroad.[9]

However, the assumptions required for worldwide taxation to be optimal do not come close to holding in the data. With nonzero taxes on the return to savings or anticipations of a possible future drop in corporate tax rates, multinationals would gain by postponing repatriation of foreign-source income and letting this income accrue in a tax haven. The data show that multinationals have indeed built up large holdings of profits abroad, concentrated in tax havens.[10] Given this behavior, foreign-source income under worldwide taxation has, in practice, largely been exempt from domestic corporate taxes, as it would be under a territorial tax. Yet worldwide taxation still distorts behavior, by inducing firms to defer repatriations. A territorial tax may then seem second-best.

A territorial tax is very second-best, though, since it introduces a variety of large tax distortions. While purely domestic firms face full corporate taxation of their profits, multinationals can easily avoid corporate taxes by shifting their profits into tax havens. Multinationals not only can avoid tax on their foreign-source income but can also enable owners and workers to shift their income from the firm's domestic operations out of the personal tax base into the domestic corporate tax base and then to shift this income abroad into a tax haven, thereby avoiding taxes even on their domestic-source income. This ease of international income shifting seriously undermines the income tax as a whole.

It is clear that the income tax has been under substantial pressures. The average marginal corporate tax rate among OECD countries has halved since 1980.[11] This cut in corporate tax rates creates pressures to cut personal tax rates as well, to lessen the distortions favoring income shifting from the personal into the corporate tax base. There is no obvious floor on these corporate and personal tax rates, except to

---

[7] Note, though, that "worldwide taxes" do not allow an immediate deduction when funds are shifted abroad, only a tax-free repatriation of this initial investment when the funds are finally repatriated.

[8] This finding is analogous to the result that the rate of return earned on funds invested in a pension plan simply equals the pretax market interest rate.

[9] When the host country imposes a tax on the subsidiary, perhaps to discourage domestic income shifting between the firm and its workers, then the home country only needs to impose a tax net of a credit for taxes paid abroad to discourage international income shifting.

[10] See Tørsløv et al. (2018) for evidence.

[11] See Slemrod (2018).

the degree that there are real costs from engaging in this income shifting. Costs are likely to be low.

Section 4 then explores alternatives to the current design of existing corporate and personal income taxes. One alternative, proposed in Auerbach et al. (2010), is a cash-flow corporate tax. Such a tax shares the strengths but also many of the weaknesses described above for "worldwide taxation," since it still induces firms to retain funds abroad when there is a nonzero tax on the return to savings under the personal tax or anticipations of a future cut in the corporate tax rate.

Another option that has been under long-standing discussion within the European Union (EU) is the use of formula apportionment as a means of allocating a firm's worldwide profits among different countries, as is done by US states when allocating a firm's US profits across states. The main advantage of this approach is that worldwide profits are not affected by income shifting across locations. There are many disadvantages, though, as described in section 3.

The third option we consider is to shift to a consumption tax base under the personal tax. The need for the corporate tax arose because corporate income is treated more favorably than noncorporate income (or wages and salaries) under the existing personal tax,[12] opening up incentives to convert noncorporate income as well as wages and salaries into corporate income. Yet income held in registered accounts,[13] e.g. pension plans, is treated the same regardless of whether it accrues within corporate or noncorporate firms or from domestic of foreign-source activity. If any securities vulnerable to income shifting must be held in a registered account, then the personal tax would itself avoid any distortions to the location of economic activity and (to that extent) achieve productive efficiency. There would then be no need for a corporate tax. Indeed any such tax would introduce distortions.

Section 5 then turns to tax enforcement and other omissions from the discussion in Section 3. The prior theory assumed that the government can successfully monitor the desired tax base. In theory, the government can choose an intensity of tax audits and a level of fines due when evasion is detected that should be sufficient to deter evasion. But available data suggest a nontrivial informal economy even in the richest countries and a major understatement of taxable profits particularly by smaller firms in the formal sector. A recent literature tries to understand better how to redesign the corporate tax to lessen these evasion pressures.

Section 6 focuses on several of the market failures suggested by the past empirical literature examining corporate behavior and considers how the

---

[12] This is largely due to the favorable tax treatment of accruing capital gains.

[13] Under a registered account, any funds added to the account to acquire new securities are deductible from taxable income that year but all withdrawals from the registered account are fully taxable.

corporate tax might be used to lessen the efficiency costs arising from these market failures.

Finally, section 7 provides a brief summary of this Element.

2 Effects of Taxes on Corporate Behavior

2.1 Overview

Corporate behavior will ultimately depend on all of the tax implications of decisions firms might make, not only from the corporate income tax but also from the personal income tax. The focus in this section will be on how these two layers of tax combine to affect key corporate decisions.[14]

Largely, these two layers of tax have been designed so that income is taxed either under the corporate tax or under the personal tax but not both. In particular, most payouts from the corporate sector (dividends aside) are deductible from the corporate tax base but are then taxable under the personal tax, whether these payouts take the form of wages, bonuses, rents, royalties, or interest payments.

Of course, there are exceptions. Fringe benefits are a broad category of payments that are deductible under the corporate tax but not taxable under the personal tax. Here, though, there is a cap on the size of these payouts.

The main exception is dividends, where dividend payouts are not deductible under the corporate tax but taxable in some form under the personal income tax, discouraging dividend payments. Most countries, though, have added statutory provisions weakening this higher effective tax rate on dividends. One approach is through the use of dividend imputation schemes that give individuals a credit for the presumed corporate taxes paid on the income financing these dividends. Another is either a reduced corporate tax rate on income paid out as dividends or a reduced personal tax rate on dividend income.

Beyond these distortions to dividend payments, to the extent that the combined effective tax rate from both corporate taxes plus any personal taxes due on corporate income differs from the personal tax rate faced by those receiving payouts from the firm, there are distortions concerning where income is reported.[15] As seen throughout the rest of section 2, many aspects of corporate behavior are affected.

In discussing the impact of taxes on each type of corporate behavior, we start with a theoretical description of the incentives created by the tax law, assuming

---

[14] For an overlapping list of the economic distortions associated with the corporate tax, see Dharmapala (2016).

[15] Personal taxes due on corporate income include not only those paid on dividends but also those paid on the capital gains on corporate equity (when realized) generated from retentions.

a neoclassical setting with well-functioning markets and profit-maximizing firms. We then shift to look at some of the past empirical work that examines how firms respond to these tax incentives.

2.2 Choice of Organizational Form

The most basic distortion created by a corporate tax is to discourage firms from incorporating.[16] There are a variety of legal forms of ownership for a firm, with specific choices varying over time and across countries. To begin with, a firm can incorporate and be subject to the corporate tax, with some personal taxes then due on any dividend receipts from the firm or on any realized capital gains when shares in the firm are ultimately sold. Denote the taxable income of the firm by Y and the corporate tax rate by τ. Denote the weighted average personal tax rate on dividend receipts (weighting by shares owned) by t_d, the anticipated present value of taxes on realized capital gains due per dollar of retained earnings by g, and the fraction of after-corporate-tax profits paid out as dividends by f. A conventional measure of the resulting after-tax income then equals $Y(1 - \tau)(1 - t_e) \equiv Y(1 - \tau^*)$, where $t_e = ft_d + (1 - f)g$ and where τ^* denotes the overall combined tax rate on corporate income.

Alternatively, the firm can operate under one of a variety of "pass-through" organizational forms, where each owner's share of the firm's income is included directly in their personal taxable income.[17] Denote the weighted average personal tax rate of the shareholders in any given firm by m (weighting by share ownership). Assuming the firm's pretax income is unaffected by this choice of legal form of ownership, after-tax income if the firm chooses a "pass-through" form of ownership would instead equal $Y(1 - m)$.

Forecasted behavior is then stark. Profit-maximizing firms with $Y > 0$ would choose a pass-through form whenever $\tau^* > m$, and conversely. In years when the top corporate rate exceeds a weighted average across all shareholders of their personal tax rate, this initial theory implies that any firm with diversified ownership that would be subject to the top corporate tax rate should choose instead a pass-through form. Yet, according to the data, even in years when the corporate rate was higher than the top personal tax rate, corporations still constituted a major fraction of the economy.

This puzzle is only strengthened when we include as well the choices made by firms expecting to face tax losses. Until 2018, in the United States, owners of pass-through firms could deduct any losses from their other personal income,

---

[16] Our summary of this literature is drawn from MacKie-Mason and Gordon (1997), and Goolsbee (1998).

[17] In the United States, pass-through forms include partnerships, proprietorships, limited-liability companies, and subchapter S corporations.

saving taxes that year in proportion to their tax rate m.[18] In contrast, owners of corporate firms accruing tax losses can only use these losses to offset that firm's taxes during the previous three years (tax-loss carrybacks) or to offset future tax payments in any of the next fifteen years (tax-loss carryforwards). When tax savings from losses are deferred, their present value falls, and disappears if the firm fails prior to making full use of these tax-loss carryforwards. Prior to 2018, firms expecting tax losses were then far more likely to save taxes by choosing a pass-through form than firms expecting to earn profits.

Clearly there is some nontax factor favoring the corporate form, at least for large firms.[19] One important attribute of a corporation is limited liability for the firm's shareholders. Individual owners of a partnership or proprietorship, in contrast, are personally liable for any losses that the firm may incur. As argued by Jensen and Meckling (1976), limited liability makes it easier to sell shares in the firm, since the worst outcome outside investors might face is a total loss of their initial investment in the firm, whereas investors in a partnership or proprietorship face no cap to the losses they might incur, forcing them to check much more extensively for possible hidden liabilities of the firm. In contrast, lenders to such a firm are better protected than lenders to a corporate firm since they can seek repayment not only from the firm's assets but also from the assets of each of the individual shareholders in the firm. The data show that small firms rely on debt finance much more heavily than larger firms, making outside finance easier for smaller firms if they choose to be noncorporate. In contrast, large firms rely much more heavily on equity finance and would therefore gain by choosing to be corporate.

The limited liability available to corporations, though, is not sufficient in itself to explain the large size of the corporate sector. Limited-liability companies and subchapter S firms also face limited liability, providing a readily available way to maintain limited liability yet avoid the corporate tax.

Another factor favoring the corporate form of ownership is the greater ease of trading corporate than noncorporate shares. When a corporate shareholder sells their shares, the only consequence is that future dividend payments are now sent to the new owner. When owners of a pass-through firm (e.g. a partner in a law firm) sell shares, the sales contract needs to specify how the firm's income for that tax year will be divided between the prior and the new owner. The firm also has to refile its ownership papers with the State, documenting its new ownership pattern. Noncorporate shares also, with rare exceptions, cannot be publicly traded. Given these heavier administrative costs for trading shares in a noncorporate firm, these

---

[18] As of 2018, noncorporate firms can only carry losses forward to offset any future profits.

[19] Given the progressive corporate tax schedule in the United States, small corporations can face a much lower corporate tax rate, potentially providing a net tax advantage from being corporate.

firms typically have few owners, likely imposing high risk-bearing costs on these owners from the firm's idiosyncratic risks.

The easiest way to proceed in empirical work has been to assume that the pretax certainty-equivalent income of a corporate firm differs from the pretax income of a noncorporate firm by some amount G, with G varying by firm. The presumption is that G is positive (favoring the corporate form) to the extent that the firm is larger or riskier but potentially negative when the firm is small. The corporate form is then favored for profitable firms to the extent that $(Y + G)(1 - \tau^*) > Y(1 - m)$, or equivalently to the extent that:

$$\frac{G}{Y} > \frac{\tau^* - m}{1 - \tau^*} \tag{1}$$

Note that the tax law creates no distortion to this decision when $\tau^* = m$, a result we will see repeatedly throughout the rest of section 2.

Given some distribution for G/Y among firms in an industry, this equation forecasts the fraction of firms that will choose to be corporate as a function of the tax expression on the right-hand side of equation (1). In principle, these tax rates vary by firm, given a progressive corporate tax schedule and idiosyncratic ownership patterns across firms. Past empirical work, though, has largely used time series variation.[20] While tax rate changes do lead to some variation in ownership patterns in the direction expected, estimated behavioral responses in the past literature are small, suggesting that nontax factors dominate this particular decision.

2.2.1 Notes on the Determinants of the Effective Capital Gains Tax Rate

The statutory capital gains tax rate g has always been no higher than t_d. But taxes due on accruing gains are deferred until the stock is ultimately sold and the gains are realized. In addition, investors have an incentive to realize any capital losses quickly, in order to get immediate tax savings on these capital losses.[21] In the United States, the capital gains on shares still unsold at death escape capital gains tax entirely due to a write-up of basis at death, giving individuals an incentive to include assets with large unrealized capital gains as part of their estate. Given the tax savings from capital losses and the deferral of taxes on

---

[20] One important issue here is that marginal tax rates depend on the reported level of taxable income, while reported income can also depend on the tax rate the firm faces, raising endogeneity concerns in measuring the tax expression in equation (1). Papers vary in the types of instrumentation used. The easiest approach is to use the top statutory tax rates as instruments.

[21] If capital losses are realized quickly enough to represent short-term losses, then the tax savings are larger as well as quicker.

capital gains (or avoidance entirely through a write-up of basis), there is no assurance that the effective tax rate is even positive. While a rule of thumb, dating to a paper by Feldstein et al. (1983), is that the effective capital gains rate is roughly a quarter of the statutory tax rate on long-term gains, halved due to deferral and halved again due to a write-up of basis at death, there have been no careful studies looking at actual patterns of realizations and their implications for the effective capital gains tax rate.

2.2.2 Notes on the Determinants of t_e

In section 2.2 we set $t_e = ft_d + (1 - f)g$. According to the data, publicly traded firms have, in the past, paid out roughly half of their profits in dividends. Note, though, that a firm maximizing after-tax profits would set $f = 0$, since $g < t_d$, and then use any excess cash flow to repurchase shares rather than pay dividends. This conflict between theory and data has been a long-standing puzzle in the corporate finance literature, as emphasized in Black (1976). Various theories have been proposed to explain why firms pay dividends in spite of the tax disadvantage of doing so.[22] These include "the new view," signaling models in which dividends convey information to outside shareholders, and agency models in which shareholders use dividends to constrain the budget of the firm's manager.

The "new view" was proposed in King (1977), Auerbach (1979), and Bradford (1981). An implicit assumption in the above discussion was that the increase in share values in response to a dollar of extra retained earnings is a dollar. In a commonly used notation, the assumption is that $q = 1$ where (Tobin's) q is the ratio of the market value of the firm to its book value. The market equilibrium would indeed be $q = 1$ if the firm could sell or repurchase shares whenever this equality did not hold. The "new view," though, assumes that firms cannot repurchase shares. Without this option of repurchasing shares, q can well fall below 1.

Tobin's q cannot fall too far, though, because the firm would choose to pay dividends rather than invest whenever $1 - m \geq q(1 - g)$. Let $q^* = (1 - m)/(1 - q)$ represent the value of q where the firm is just indifferent to paying dividends. Firms can then be in one of three different regimes: (1) $q = 1$, where they sell shares to maintain this equality but never pay dividends; (2) $1 > q > q^*$, where firms neither issue shares nor pay dividends; and (3) $q = q^*$, where this equality is maintained through the choice of a dividend payout rate.

---

[22] The discussion in this section draws heavily on the analysis in Gordon and Dietz (2008).

One striking implication of this theory is that the dividend tax, while lowering the value of firms, does not affect investment incentives for firms in the third regime. To see this, note that, if the firm pays a dollar in dividends now, shareholders receive q^*. If instead, the firm retains the dollar and invests it, earning an after-corporate-tax return of ρ, and then pays this return out in dividends the next period, investors receive $q^*\rho$. Their rate of return from the deferred payout $(q^*\rho/q^*)$ is then ρ and is unaffected by the dividend tax rate. Given that the tax does not affect investment, by the firm's budget constraint dividends are unaffected as well. The tax on dividends does discourage new share issues, though.

The "New View" faces many challenges. The key added assumption is that firms cannot repurchase shares. Yet repurchases by US firms are certainly feasible and expenditures on repurchases have been growing steadily in importance in the United States over time and are now larger than aggregate dividend payments.[23] In some countries, such as the UK, repurchases are indeed banned by law. But, in that case, firms have an incentive to acquire shares in other firms whenever $q < 1$, since this allows a firm to buy the assets held by the firm at a cheaper price than it would face buying these assets directly. Acquisitions replace share repurchases as a way to avoid dividend taxes. There are no legal restrictions preventing acquisitions.

The theory also makes a variety of counterfactual forecasts. For one, the theory forecasts that firms issuing new shares should never pay dividends. Yet this is often seen in the data. Dividend payout rates are remarkably stable over time; however, the theory forecasts that dividends should be very volatile, since they equal the difference between after-tax cash flow and investment expenditures, both of which are volatile.

Past studies also find that announcements of new dividend payments cause share prices to rise. Under the "new view," though, firms paying dividends should face $q = q^*$, implying that investors should be indifferent between an extra dollar of dividends or having the funds retained, invested, and then paid out in the future.

A second proposed explanation for dividends, motivated by this effect of dividends on share prices, is that dividends are being used by managers to signal to the market the firm's (otherwise unobserved) cash flow.[24]

For outside investors to infer something about the firm's cash flow from the payout decisions of the manager, they must understand the manager's objective

---

[23] For evidence, see Grullon-Michaely (2002).
[24] See, e.g., Miller and Rock (1985), Bernheim (1991) and Bernheim and Wantz (1995).

function and already know all elements entering this objective function other than the unobserved cash flow.

Assume that the manager currently owns h shares and plans to sell s percent of them in the next period, giving the manager an incentive to care about next period's share price. Based on their self-interest, the manager would choose the dividend payout rate to maximize:[25]

$$shV_{market} + (1 - s)hV_{true} + (1 - t^*)hD, \tag{2}$$

where $1 - t^* \equiv (1 - m)/(1 - g)$ captures the tax disadvantage of dividends relative to capital gains received on the firm's shares, V_{market} denotes the firm's share value based on the information available to outside shareholders, V_{true} denotes the firm's share value based on the information available to the manager, while D represents the dividends paid on each share.

For the manager's choice of the dividend payout rate to reveal information about the firm's cash flow, denoted by F, the effects of the payout rate on V_{true} must depend on F. Assume that

$$\frac{\partial V_{true}}{\partial D} = -1 - C(F - D). \tag{3}$$

Here, the function $C(.)$ is a nonnegative negatively sloped convex function that asymptotes to zero. It measures the cost the firm faces from a more binding cash-flow constraint when it starts with only $F - D$ available for operating purposes. Intuitively, firms with substantial cash flow can easily afford a higher payout rate ($C \approx 0$), whereas firms with limited cash flow must forego potentially valuable projects in order to finance a higher payout rate.

The resulting first-order condition is

$$sh\frac{\partial V_{market}}{\partial D} = (1 - s)h(1 + C(F - D)) - h(1 - t^*). \tag{4}$$

Outside investors are assumed to know all elements of this equation except F. Based on equation (4), they can then back out F as a function of D. In equilibrium, $\partial V_{market}/\partial D$ then equals the inferred value for $\partial V_{true}/\partial D$.

There are various complications that have been added to this model. Chetty and Saez (2010) find empirically that tax cuts lead to a smaller increase in dividends for firms where managers own options on the firm's stocks rather than owning the stock outright. The key difference between options and the firm's underlying stock is that owners of an option do not receive dividends paid out

---

[25] If s = 1, then all managers make the same choice and the payout rate cannot reveal any information, whereas if s = 0 then the manager has no reason to try to affect the market price for the firm's shares.

prior to the date when the option is exercised. Compensating managers through options then makes dividends less attractive to a manager.

One important implicit assumption in the above model is that dividends serve as the signal of the firm's true profits. Why not signal through repurchases instead, which have the advantage that the resulting capital gains face a lower tax rate? Bernheim and Wantz (1995) made the choice between repurchases and dividends explicit and assume that the firm chooses an overall payout P to shareholders that is β percent dividends and $(1 - \beta)$ percent repurchases. Now the last term in equation (2) becomes $(1 - \beta t^*)hP$. For any given β, the solution proceeds as before. But β can then be chosen ex ante to maximize the equilibrium value of equation (2). Using a larger share of repurchases in the firm's payouts saves on taxes, of course. However, the solution to equation (4) involves higher equilibrium payouts when the taxes due on payouts are lower. These higher equilibrium payouts raise the firm's real costs $C(F - P)$.

Implicitly, there is an optimal value of β, trading off the marginal cost of the signal with the equilibrium size of the signal. One striking result is that any change in the tax rate on dividends will lead to a compensating adjustment to β so as to leave the overall cost of the signal, and the overall payout rate, unchanged.

This updated theory can certainly explain the existence of both dividend payouts and simultaneous repurchases from a firm. Either version can explain why share prices go up when the announced payouts are higher.

But some inconsistencies with the data still remain. For example, past studies find that share prices fall in response to an increase in the tax rate on dividends, a finding contrary to the forecasts from this model.[26]

The data also show that dividend payout rates are remarkably stable but also show that the amount spent on share repurchases is extremely volatile.[27] Yet the above theory assumes the two move proportionately.

The Appendix contains a sketch of a possible extension of this signaling model in which dividends signal the manager's longer-run expectations for the firm's cash flow. What is key in supporting this alternative model is an assumed penalty in the manager's compensation scheme whenever the dividend payout rate is cut, a penalty used to induce managers to reveal their longer-run expectations. The stability of dividends in itself then need not overturn a signaling model.[28]

---

[26] For one such study, see Auerbach and Hassett (2006).

[27] For evidence, see, e.g., Chetty and Saez (2006).

[28] Repurchases instead can signal an unusually high one-period jump in the firm's cash flow. Signaling both expected cash flow and its value period-by-period requires two instruments.

A third approach to explain dividends uses an agency model, in which managers are empire builders, wanting to invest more than is in the interests of shareholders, perhaps because managers overseeing firms with more capital command higher salaries.[29] The firm's board of directors, acting in the interests of shareholders, can then use dividend payouts to reduce the firm's "free cash-flow," with the aim of limiting the funds available to the manager to the amount that would finance the rate of investment that is in the interest of the share-holders. In this model, the board rather than the manager controls the dividend payout rate, based on the information it has available, which should be better than that available to shareholders but less good than that available to the manager.

The challenge faced by the board is that the firm's internal cash flow is volatile and not easily monitored even by the board of directors given the flexibility available to the manager in putting together the firm's financial statements. The board must then choose a payout rate trading off the costs of too low a payout rate if ex post profits are high with the costs of too high a payout rate if ex post profits are low.

For most outcomes for ex post profits, by design the board has left managers with a tight enough budget that they will simply use the available funds for the most valuable projects. However, if ex post profits are high enough to cover even the higher investment rate preferred by the manager, then the manager gains from using any further profits to repurchase shares. In contrast, if ex post profits are low enough, then the manager would find it worth the assumed costs to issue new shares, even recognizing the resulting negative signal to outside investors about the firm's current cash flow.

As a result, this framework can explain the potentially simultaneous presence of dividends and repurchases or of dividends and new share issues. It also easily explains why share prices jump in response to dividend and repurchase announcements and fall in response to announced new share issues.

It can go some way to explaining why dividend payout rates are so stable. Payout rates are chosen by the board, who cannot easily monitor the firm's actual profit rate, so must base their decisions on information that changes only slowly over time. The board can certainly see repurchases and new share issues, though, occasionally giving it new information about the firm's profit rate (and rate of investment). In itself, this new information should lead to an increase in the board's choice for the dividend payout rate in the next period. However, such an increase in the future dividend payout rate would make managers worse

---

[29] The specific details used here come from Gordon and Dietz (2008). Chetty and Saez (2010) also develop an agency model of dividends, though without the uncertainty in cash flow that can be used to explain the payout of dividends by firms that also repurchase shares or issue new shares.

off. As a result, managers would face an incentive to forego repurchases (using the funds for a yet higher rate of investment) and new stock issues (accepting too low investment), in order to avoid giving the board any justification for increasing the firm's payout rate. Recognizing this adverse incentive created for the manager from the board's flexibility in setting the dividend payout rate, the board would gain from committing to limit this flexibility, leading to a yet more stable dividend payout rate.

The key question faced in this model, though, is why the board does not use repurchases rather than dividends to limit the manager's free cash flow. Both are equally effective in limiting the manager's free cash flow. One possible explanation: If both the board and the manager can decide on share repurchases, then outside shareholders face a challenge in inferring anything about the state of the firm, not knowing whose information and incentives led to the choice of a payout rate.

In the rest of the discussion, we sidestep this debate and simply interpret g as the effective personal tax rate on corporate income net of the corporate tax.

2.3 Taxes and the Choice of Debt vs. Equity Finance

To the extent that $\tau^* \neq m$, firms face an incentive to shift taxable income between the firm and its shareholders in order to save jointly on taxes. There are many ways of doing this.

Probably the largest literature on such income shifting focuses on the firm's choice between debt and equity finance.[30] Consider the tax implications of a firm selling another dollar of equity in the financial market and then using the proceeds to retire a dollar of loans from these same shareholders. Corporate tax payments now go up by $i\tau$, where i is the nominal interest rate on the firm's debt. Shareholders now accrue extra income of $(1 - \tau)i$ on which their effective tax rate is g but save taxes of im since they no longer receive interest on the debt that was retired.[31] Taxes discourage this choice to the extent that $(\tau^* - m)i > 0$. For firms in the top corporate tax bracket, this expression is typically strongly positive, in part because loans often come from tax-exempt savings.

On tax grounds, then, debt finance is preferred to equity finance. To what degree do nontax factors enter as well? A seminal paper by Modigliani and Miller (1958) argued that (ignoring taxes, real bankruptcy costs, or other market failures) firms should be indifferent to their choice of debt vs. equity finance.

---

[30] See Graham (2003) for an overview of the literature on taxes and corporate finance.

[31] Here, m represents the implicit tax rate on interest income embodied in market prices. See Gordon and Bradford (1980) for a derivation showing that this should be a weighted average of the tax rates among investors, with wealthier and less risk-averse investors receiving more weight.

Regardless of how the firm divides its overall payouts between dividends, share repurchases, and interest payments, investors can allocate the resulting risks and returns efficiently among themselves through their portfolio choices, so that the choice of financial policy has no real consequences. Given a tax distortion favoring debt finance, Miller and Modigliani (1963) then argue that firms should be *entirely* debt financed.

Yet, according to US data, the aggregate debt/asset ratio among profitable corporations is only about 25 percent, indicating that some nontax factors must be playing a dominant role in corporate finance decisions among these firms. But what are these nontax factors? The obvious first place to focus is real costs of bankruptcy: As the firm raises its use of debt, the chance of default goes up, leading to a higher probability of facing any real costs of bankruptcy. A high enough incremental cost would counterbalance the tax savings from use of debt.

The problem with this hypothesis is that attempts to measure real bankruptcy costs suggest they are an order of magnitude smaller that the potential tax savings from additional use of debt.[32] This bankruptcy-cost hypothesis also implies that firms with tax losses should not use debt finance, since doing so is discouraged on tax grounds and raises (more than for other firms) the chance of facing real costs of bankruptcy. Yet firms with tax losses certainly make active use of debt finance.

Perhaps the offsetting costs occur outside of bankruptcy, arising from the conflicts of interest between debt and equity holders. For example, the firm acting in the interests of equity holders may pursue riskier projects than would be in the interests of debt and equity holders together. Lenders would then charge higher interest rates ex ante in anticipation of such behavior. Here, it is harder to judge empirically whether these overall real costs of debt are sufficient to explain the limited use of debt seen in the data.

An alternative hypothesis, appearing in Myers and Majluf (1983), is that firms choosing to borrow face a lemons problem. Under this hypothesis, outside investors know less about the true value of the firm than the firm's manager and try to infer the true value of the firm from the manager's actions.

When the firm borrows a dollar, the market interest rate it faces depends on investors' expectations regarding the chance of default on these loans and the amount recovered in the event of default. If a given firm were to borrow an amount I sufficient to finance some new project, denote the interest rate charged, given market expectations, by r_m. In contrast, denote the interest (as

---

[32] For one source of data on bankruptcy costs, see White (1983).

perceived by the manager) at which outside lenders would just break even by r^*. With symmetric information, the project should be pursued if its return is at least r^*I. Denote the rate of return as perceived given the information of the manager as $r^*I + X$. Debt finance of the project is then in the interests of the firm only if $X > (r_m - r^*)I$. For any given project, only firms with r^* above some cutoff $r^c = r_m - X/I$ will choose to proceed with this debt-financed project. The market interest rate, r_m, then reflects the inference that only weaker firms (those with $r^* > r^c$) will issue debt. Better firms will either forego such projects or proceed with internal funds.

If the firm instead finances the project with new equity issues, it still gains $r^*I + X$ from the project. From the perspective of the manager, though, the rate of return demanded by shareholders equals r^*IS/P, where S is the manager's perceived value of a share, whereas P is the value per share perceived by the market. Only firms with $S < P\left(1 + \frac{X}{r^*I}\right)$ will proceed with the project financed with new equity issues, with P set based on this inference. Again, better firms either forego the project or finance it with internal funds.

Outcomes as a result are inefficient, given that some of the better firms will forego these projects and others will face a higher internal opportunity cost due to these lemons problems. There would be less of a lemons problem with debt than with equity, since only asymmetric information about the lower tail of the distribution of true values for the firm matter for debt but the full distribution matters for equity. Asymmetric information then favors debt finance over equity finance but market interest rates can be sufficiently high that better firms choose not to borrow.

To the extent that $\tau^* > m$, taxes induce more firms to borrow and those that do borrow potentially undertake more ambitious projects. There is a large past literature estimating the degree to which a firm's debt/equity ratio responds to the tax incentives it faces, where the net tax savings from a shift of a dollar of finance from equity to debt equals $i(\tau^* - m)$. Most papers have focused on the tax expression in parentheses and ignored the interest rate term. Gordon and Lee (2007), though, used the full expression for the tax savings from an extra dollar of debt in their empirical work. Potential endogeneity of this tax expression is always a concern, since more profitable firms would face a higher marginal corporate tax rate and a lower interest rate, yet would likely borrow less for nontax reasons. As a result, this and other studies instrument for the tax expression, in this case using government bond rates for the interest rate and the statutory marginal corporate tax rate that would be expected given the size of the firm's assets and typical taxable rates of return. The empirical evidence shows some clear responsiveness of a firm's capital structure to taxes.

2.4 Other Forms of Income Shifting

Given the limited use of debt finance to shift income between the corporate and the personal tax bases, corporations (and their shareholders) face strong incentives to find other means of shifting income between these two tax bases. There are many strategies that might be pursued, particularly in closely held firms.

For one, firms can compensate workers in multiple ways. When firms pay employees (or managers) with equity, by US statute the market value of this equity compensation is a deductible expense for the firm and taxable income to the employees. For closely held firms, though, the equity is not publicly traded, hence there is no objective measure of its market value. In the United States, the Internal Revenue Service (IRS) has given closely held firms substantial discretion in assigning a value to this equity, discretion that can be used to shift taxable income from higher to lower tax rates.[33] Another alternative in the United States for compensation is use of qualified options. In the United States, these options are neither a deductible expense to the firm nor taxable income to the employee. Use of these options is then attractive when the firm's effective corporate tax rate is low relative to that employee's personal tax rate.

Other strategies often involve one or another form of tax evasion, though ones that are hard to detect. For example, whenever shareholders lend money to the firm, they could set artificial interest rates on these loans, thereby shifting income from higher to lower tax rates. Similarly, shareholders can personally buy the corporation's building or equipment and lease this capital to the firm at an artificial rent. Shareholders (rather than the firm) can own key patents and then manipulate the royalties charged for use of this intellectual property (or the sales price for the patent if it is traded between these two parties).

When firms pay wages to workers, this is a deductible expense for the firm and taxable income to the employees. On net, the firm and any given worker gain from reporting these payments when the effective corporate tax rate exceeds the personal tax rate of that worker.[34] But, when the effective corporate tax rate is less than the personal tax rate of that worker, there is a joint tax incentive to avoid wage payments, either by simply not reporting this income or else by finding other forms of compensation that face a more favorable tax treatment.

---

[33] For example, start-up firms without taxable income for some period can compensate workers with stock in the firm rather than with wages and then assign a trivial par value to these shares. The resulting tax savings to the workers can dramatically outweigh any tax costs to the firm from having lower tax-loss carryforwards when and if it becomes profitable.

[34] This tax incentive likely explains why third-party reporting by firms of the taxable labor income of the firm's employees seems to be so accurate.

How much of this income shifting occurs? The incentive for such income shifting again depends on the differences in effective tax rates: $\tau^* - m$, where m is now the marginal tax rate of a particular employee. To estimate the responsiveness of income shifting to these tax incentives, Gordon and Slemrod (2000) looked at how corporate profits before interest deductions, as a fraction of corporate assets, depend on this tax differential.[35] The results show that, when corporate tax rates are relatively high, corporations report a significantly lower rate of return, the opposite of what would be expected given the presumption of a higher required pretax rate of return for corporate investments when the corporate tax rate is higher. More strikingly, reported corporate rates of return increase when personal tax rates rise, an effect that is hard to explain other than through income shifting.

Income shifting should show up for the same reasons in the personal tax base. One place to focus is the reported rate of return to noncorporate firms. Noncorporate firms owned by individuals in a personal tax bracket above the corporate tax rate would gain by acquiring activities that run a tax loss and then selling these activities back to the corporate sector when and if they generate taxable profits. An example would be oil and gas drilling. Firms in this industry have commonly been run as a partnership during the drilling phase, when there are heavy expenses but no current income, with losses immediately deductible against other personal income. If and when oil or gas is discovered, the business can be sold to a corporate firm, generating taxable capital gains for the partnership, with future income taxed at the lower corporate tax rate. One striking documentation for such income shifting is the observation that the aggregate income of the noncorporate sector as a whole shifted from being sharply negative prior to the 1986 Tax Reform Act to being sharply positive after the Act reduced even the top personal tax rate below the new corporate tax rate.

This evidence for income shifting could in part reflect intertemporal shifting of the timing of taxable compensation to years when individual rates are relatively low relative to corporate rates.[36] An easy way to do this in the United States is through providing compensation in the form of nonqualified options. When employees are compensated using nonqualified options, there are no resulting tax deductions or taxable income except in the year (if ever) when the option is exercised. In that year, the difference between the market value of the shares received and the strike price of these shares is a deductible expense for the firm and taxable income to the employee. Employees can build

---

[35] By looking at profits prior to interest deductions, income shifting through use of debt is left out of the study. By looking at profits per dollar of assets, the potential effect of taxes on corporate investment or on corporate/noncorporate choices will also be neutralized.

[36] See Goolsbee (2000) and Gorry et al. (2017) for empirical evidence.

up a stock of these unexercised options and then exercise the accumulated stock whenever the corporate tax rate is unusually high compared to the employee's personal tax rate. Similarly, when firms provide defined-benefit pensions to workers, the firm can make an immediate deduction for payments used to fund these future pensions, whereas workers are taxed on the resulting pension income only during retirement when their personal tax rate is relatively low.

Income shifting not only occurs between the corporate and personal tax bases within a country but also between countries. This income shifting can take many forms. The most obvious is within a multinational, where reported taxable income can be shifted to subsidiaries in low-tax countries (or even tax havens with no tax), while expenses can be shifted to the subsidiaries facing the highest statutory tax rate. One method for shifting income among subsidiaries is transfer pricing: The prices assigned to goods traded between subsidiaries of a multinational can be manipulated in order to shift taxable profits from subsidiaries facing a high tax rate to ones facing a low tax rate. In principle, firms are supposed to use "arm's-length" prices for these transactions but many goods (and particularly services) are only exchanged within that multinational, e.g. managerial services, giving the firm great discretion in assigning a transfer price for these goods.

Another form of manipulation by multinationals is to have a subsidiary in a low-tax country own the patents on new technology, even though the research and development (R&D) was done elsewhere, and then charge high royalty rates for use of the intellectual property. There is empirical evidence that multinationals also have their subsidiaries in high-tax countries do the bulk of the borrowing for the multinational as a whole and then use the resulting funds to make equity investments in other parts of the business.[37]

Available data suggest that the extent of income shifting is dramatic. According to the data in Tørsløv et al. (2018), tax haven affiliates are on average five times more profitable than nonhaven affiliates. If there were no income shifting, then firms should report a pretax corporate profit rate in any given country c equal to $\rho/(1 - \tau_c)$, in order to provide the going (certainty-equivalent) net-of-corporate-tax rate of return ρ required by the global financial market. The forecast, ignoring income shifting, is then a lower pretax profit rate in countries with a lower corporate tax rate. The data strongly show the opposite pattern, with very low profit rates in the highest-tax countries and enormous reported rates of return in tax havens.

---

[37] See Gordon and Hines (2002) for a review of this literature and Grubert (2003) for evidence on the extent to which each of these income-shifting methods have been used by multinationals.

Even among unrelated firms, firms in high-tax countries can pursue activities that generate low taxable income while those in low-tax countries can pursue activities that face high effective tax rates: Taxes affect a country's comparative advantage, both over final goods and over the location of each stage of production. Firms can also simply engage in paper transactions to shift income. As an example, if one country offers unusually generous depreciation provisions, then firms in that country can on paper buy capital to be used in firms located in countries with less generous provisions and then lease the capital to these firms, with the lease rate reflecting the resulting tax savings.

2.5 Taxes and Rates of Corporate Investment: Closed Economy Case

In laying out the effects of taxes on rates of corporate investment, we start with the simplest of settings: a static model with firms always corporate, no risk, 100 percent equity finance, stable prices, and no credit constraints.

To set up notation, assume to begin with that there are no taxes. A firm is considering an additional dollar of investment in a unit of capital that is assumed to face exponential depreciation at a rate d in the value of that capital relative to available replacements. Investments elsewhere earn a pretax (real) rate of return equal to r. A unit of output is defined so that its price is a dollar while f_K is the value of the marginal product of an extra dollar's work of capital. The firm just breaks even on this new investment if the net return, $f_K - d$, just covers the opportunity cost of funds, r: $f_K - d = r$.

How does this first-order condition change when we take taxes into account? One complication is how to take into account the depreciation deductions allowed under the tax law. These deductions are spread over time, according to a complicated formula that has varied over time and varies by type of capital. The convention, dating back to Hall and Jorgenson (1967), is to summarize these deductions by their present value, denoted by z.[38] The net cost of both the original dollar of new investment and the yearly replacement investment of d dollars is reduced by the factor $(1 - \tau^* z)$ per dollar of new investment, since these investments carry with them tax savings worth $\tau^* z$ in present value. As a result, the new first-order condition is

$$f_K = \left(r(1 - m) + d \right) \frac{1 - \tau^* z}{1 - \tau^*} \tag{5}$$

Here, we assume that the return on the alternative investment is fully taxable under the personal tax, as would be true for example of investments in bonds or

---

[38] These deductions should be discounted at the risk-free after-tax discount rate.

in noncorporate capital.[39] The right-hand side of this equation captures the required rate of return on a new corporate investment and is commonly referred to as the firm's user cost of capital.

Various special cases are worth noting. For one, with expensing (whereby the full cost of the investment is immediately deductible), $z = 1$. As a result, the corporate tax rate drops out of equation (5). Taxes now favor corporate investment, since the personal tax differentially affects the alternative investment, with higher personal tax rates leading to an increase in corporate investments. For taxes to be neutral, bonds should also be free of tax and noncorporate capital also expensed.

As another special case, assume that the tax law provides for "economic" depreciation, allowing (in present value) deductions worth as much as allowing d percent of the remaining capital to be deducted each period. The present value of depreciation deductions now satisfies $z = d/\left(r(1-m) + d\right)$. Substituting into equation (5) and simplifying, we find that

$$f_K = r\frac{1-m}{1-\tau^*} + d \tag{5a}$$

Taxes now drop out entirely if $\tau^* = m$, the same condition as we saw above in sections 2.2, 2.3, and 2.4 when looking at the tax distortion to the choices of organizational form, debt vs. equity finance, and other forms of income shifting. Corporate investment should go up in response to a higher personal tax rate, and drop in response to a higher corporate tax rate.

Many complications are left out of equation (5). For one, consider the choice of debt vs. equity finance. Let δ denote the fraction of the new investment financed with debt, and let $b(\delta)$ be a convex function that captures any nontax costs arising from use of bond finance for this marginal dollar of new investment. We assume that these costs are deductible under the corporate tax base. Now the first-order condition becomes

$$f_K - b(\delta) = \left[r(1-m) - \delta r(\tau^* - m) + d\right]\frac{1-\tau^* z}{1-\tau^*} \tag{5b}$$

The first-order condition for δ trades off tax savings with nontax costs. While there are no marginal savings from use of debt, there are infra-marginal savings. Firms in a better position to use debt finance, such as real estate, then face a lower user cost of capital on net.

---

[39] Throughout our discussion, we ignore any non-neutrality in the tax treatment of inflation, including the taxation of nominal interest and nominal capital gains as well as depreciation based on the nominal purchase price. See Auerbach (1981) for further discussion.

Expressions such as equation (5b), dating originally to work by King and Fullerton (1984), have formed the basis for a vast body of both policy analysis and empirical work on taxes and investment.[40] In the empirical work, the resulting summary measure is typically the right-hand side of equation (5b), the user cost of capital. In the policy analysis, the summary measure is often instead referred to as the marginal effective tax rate (METR), and defined by

$$METR = \frac{MPK - MRS}{MPK},\qquad(5c)$$

In our context, $MPK = f_K - b(\delta) - d$ measures the real pretax marginal product of capital net of depreciation, while $MRS = r(1 - m)$ is the real after-tax rate of return to savings.

Given the importance to economists of forecasting rates of investment, since investment is one of the most volatile components of the economy, there is a huge empirical literature examining rates of investment. Unavoidably, these papers control for effects of tax incentives.

Empirical studies face many challenges.[41] To begin with, the above equations characterize the equilibrium capital intensity for a firm but not its rate of investment. With the marginal product of capital expressed as a function of the firm's capital/output ratio, equation (5) can be rewritten as $f_K\left(\frac{K}{Y}\right) = c$, where c is the user cost of capital, as captured by the right-hand side of these equations. Adding subscripts for time, we now find that $K_t = f_K^{-1}(c_t)Y_t$. Investment satisfies $I_t = K_t - (1 - d)K_{t-1}$. We then infer that

$$\begin{aligned} I_t &= dK_{t-1} + f_K^{-1}(c_t)Y_t - f_K^{-1}(c_{t-1})Y_{t-1} \\ &= dK_{t-1} + Y_t\left(f_K^{-1}(c_t) - f_K^{-1}(c_{t-1})\right) + f_K^{-1}(c_{t-1})(Y_t - Y_{t-1}) \end{aligned}\qquad(6)$$

Here, the first term on the right-hand side captures replacement investment. The second term captures the effects of changes in the tax law, while the third term captures new investment needed for desired expansions in the scale of the firm.

One further challenge in empirical work is a presumption that firms face real costs in integrating new capital into the firm's ongoing operations, leading to the addition of adjustment costs of some form to this equation, perhaps of the form $A\left(\frac{I}{K}\right)$. Adjustment costs will then slow the response to new information but also lead to changes in investment in anticipation of future tax changes.

---

[40] Papers frequently add into this expression a variety of further complications, such as effects of inflation, any investment-tax credit, subsidies to particular forms of capital, wealth or property taxes, and changes in the relative prices of capital vs. output. See, e.g., Boadway et al. (1984).

[41] See Hassett and Hubbard (1997) for an overview.

When this equation is brought to the data, whether aggregate time series data or firm data sets such as Compustat, the data confirm clear effects of changes in output on rates of new investment: Firms need to acquire added capital in order to produce added output. Papers have struggled, though, to find any detectable effects of changes in the user cost on rates of investment. Why?

One inevitable problem is endogeneity. Finding appropriate instruments for the interest rate is important. In addition, a firm's actual marginal tax rate can be affected by any deductions generated as a result of new investment, making τ^* potentially endogenous as well. Statutory tax rates seem a natural instrument. But statutory tax changes can occur in response to economic conditions that also affect rates of investment.[42]

This has led to a focus on differential effects of a tax reform on different types of capital, which naturally occur when changes to depreciation schedules have differential effects across types of capital. Even if the timing of the tax change may be endogenous, there seems no reason to presume that this endogeneity should be correlated with the degree to which changes in depreciation schedules favor one type of capital vs. another, e.g. equipment vs. structures. A study focusing on these differential effects of a tax reform on different types of capital should then arguably be free of these endogeneity concerns. This is the approach taken by Cummins et al. (1994). In this setting, effects of the user cost of capital on investment do indeed show up.

There have also been a few attempts to document the presence of credit constraints limiting firm investment, perhaps due to lemons problems. One suggestive observation supporting the role of credit constraints is the strong coefficient on cash flow when cash flow is added to specifications such as equation (6). The challenge, though, is that cash flow can be a proxy for changes in demand for the firm's product, with the change in demand rather than current cash flow causing any observed correlation with investment. To try to identify a causal role of cash flow, Fazzari et al. (1988) compare results in two subsets of firms that have had real sales growth over an extended time period: The first group has had a dividend payout rate less than 10 percent while the second group has had a payout rate over 20 percent. The presumption is that the first group is likely to be liquidity constrained, whereas the second group should not be, given the flexibility it has to change its payout rate. They then add a balance sheet measure of liquidity (holdings of cash plus marketable securities) to a standard specification for investment, separately for these two subsets of the data. Liquidity matters a lot for the first subset but

---

[42] While the empirical macro literature on effects of fiscal policy on the economy has gone to great efforts to identify tax changes that are arguably "exogenous," the same concern has not to date carried over to the literature on taxes and investment.

has statistically insignificant effects for the second subset. Even if liquidity is serving as a proxy for other factors affecting investment, they hope that the bias in the estimated coefficient should be the same for these two subsets of firms, so that the difference in their coefficients provides a causal estimate of the role of liquidity constraints.

This widespread use of variants of equation (5b) in both empirical work and policy analysis ignores, though, a wide variety of complications.

One complication discussed in section 2.2.2 is how to treat taxes on dividend payouts. The conventional approach sets $\tau^* = \tau + (1 - \tau)\left(ft_d + (1 - f)g\right)$ in order to capture all taxes that appear to be due on the return to an extra dollar of investment. Yet, under the "new view" used to explain dividends, a permanent increase in the tax rate on dividends is irrelevant to investment incentives, though a temporary increase would lead to a fall in dividend payouts and an increase in investment. Under the signaling model, any change in t_d leads to an offsetting change in f so as to leave the weighted average personal tax rate unchanged. Under the agency cost model, a tax on dividends discourages the board of directors from restricting free cash flow through dividend payments, leading to an increase in investment. None of the existing theories then support the conventional measure of tax incentives.

Expressions for the user cost of capital or the METR also largely assume constant tax rates over the life of the investment. If managers expect that investment incentives will improve at some point during the useful life of a new investment, then the resulting surge in new investment following the future tax reform will drive down the future marginal product of any investment undertaken now. To compensate, the current marginal product would need to be higher to justify proceeding with the project so that the project breaks even over its useful life. Current investment then falls in anticipation of this future tax cut.

To see this formally, consider a dynamic setting where an investment decision is made at some date t, facing current tax parameters τ^* and z. The market anticipates a tax reform at date $t + k$, at which point the tax parameters will change to the new rates τ^n and z^n. The marginal product of capital will then change as of date $t + k$ so that the marginal investment breaks even at that date, implying that the present value of the returns on a dollar of capital invested at that date equals $(1 - \tau^n z^n)$. A marginal investment at date t then breaks even if

$$1 - \tau^* z = (1 - \tau^*) \int_t^{t+k} f_K e^{-\left(d + r(1-m)\right)(x-t)} dx + e^{-\left(d + r(1-m)\right)k}(1 - \tau^n z^n) \quad (5d)$$

Solving, we find that

$$f_K = \left(r(1-m)+d\right)\left(\frac{1-\tau^* z}{1-\tau^*} + e^{-\left(d+r(1-m)\right)k}\frac{\left(\tau^n z^n - \tau^* z\right)}{1-\tau^*}\right) \tag{5e}$$

To the extent that depreciation deductions become more generous in the future, then investment is discouraged now (the user cost of capital increases).

Another frequently ignored complication when characterizing corporate investment incentives is no-loss-offset provisions under the corporate tax. Under the corporate tax law, firms with losses are not per se eligible for a tax rebate as a result of this negative taxable income. In the United States, they can get a rebate of taxes paid during the previous three years and then can carry forward any remaining losses to offset taxes in any of the next fifteen years. At a minimum, the deferral of tax savings on these losses lowers the effective tax savings on these losses. Some firms may fail before using up accumulated tax-loss carryforwards. Effective tax rates rise and therefore investment incentives fall to the degree that a firm may end up with tax-loss carryforwards.[43]

A further complication ignored in the large literature calculating the user cost of capital or the METR, and the focus of this Element, is income shifting. Given the availability of both domestic income shifting (from the corporate tax base to the personal tax base of firm owners) and international income shifting (from the domestic firm to its foreign subsidiaries), firms can reduce their effective tax burden in ways ignored in this past literature.

2.6 Taxes and Rates of Corporate Investment: Open Economy Case

The above analysis of corporate investment assumed that investors face the domestic tax law for all of their investments. Cross-border investments play a major role in the economy, though, and can take the form of both portfolio investments (individual purchases of bonds and stocks issued abroad) and foreign direct investment (investments abroad by domestic firms).[44]

What changes if portfolio investment is taken into account when thinking about investment incentives? Now the firm faces some post–corporate-tax rate of return that investors worldwide require, denoted by ρ, in order to buy shares in the firm. Changes in the tax rates faced by any group of individual investors, whether domestic or foreign, should have little effect on ρ, given the many

---

[43] See Altshuler and Auerbach (1990) for an examination of the importance of tax-loss carryforwards in the data.

[44] Formally, the distinction does not depend on the identity of the purchaser but whether the purchaser ends up with less (portfolio) or more (FDI) than a 10 percent ownership share in the firm being invested in.

sources of investable funds. The first-order condition for investment would now equal

$$f_K = (\rho + d) \frac{1 - \tau z}{1 - \tau} \tag{5f}$$

One challenge here is the strong evidence for "home bias," as documented, for example, in Adler and Dumas (1983). If individual investors were simply investing worldwide to maximize their after-tax certainty-equivalent return, then they should all have well diversified portfolios of global equity, in the simplest settings even the same composition of risky assets. Yet the data show that domestic investors largely hold domestic securities and forego what would appear to be valuable international diversification. Consequently, firms are largely owned by domestic investors in the country where the firm's headquarters is located. There is a sizeable literature trying to make sense of this behavior. But the bottom line must be that equation (5) is probably a better approximation of the data than equation (5f).

What are investment incentives when a multinational based in the home country h considers investments abroad in some country, denoted by subscript a? All major countries currently have a territorial tax treatment of the resulting income, subjecting the income to corporate taxes just in the host country, so we focus on this case.[45] Proceeding mechanically, assuming economic depreciation for simplicity, the first-order condition for investment would now be

$$f_{Kha} = \frac{r}{1 - \tau_a} \left(\frac{1 - m_h}{1 - g_h} \right) + d \tag{5g}$$

The required rate of return on an investment now depends on the domestic country of the multinational undertaking the investment and is lowest for investors from the country with the lowest ratio for $(1 - m_h)/(1 - g_h)$.

If there were no limits on the ability of investors in this country to borrow abroad, then multinationals from the country with the lowest ratio for $(1 - m_h)/(1 - g_h)$ will end up owning all firms in the world, being able to break even at a lower rate of return than investors elsewhere would require.

In equilibrium, the observed average rate of return to capital should be positively correlated with τ. Yet we have already seen from Tørsløv et al. (2018) that the data show just the opposite pattern, presumably due to income shifting. If there were no limits and no costs to income shifting, then

---

[45] We return to a discussion of worldwide taxation of the income accruing to domestic multinationals in section 3.3.5.

multinationals would report all of their income in tax havens and face an effective tax rate of $\tau = 0$, regardless of the country they might invest in.

Yet purely domestic firms do face the domestic corporate tax rate in their country. Multinationals then face a tax advantage relative to domestic firms and more so the higher is the domestic corporate tax rate.

2.7 Taxes and Reported Accounting Profits

We found in the discussion of signaling models in section 2.2.2 some indirect evidence that corporate managers care not only about the true value of the firm but also its stock price period by period. This could occur in part because managerial compensation schemes can depend in part on the firm's share price. Managers also commonly own substantial stock in the firm and may plan on selling some of those shares in the near future, giving them an incentive to care about the price for these shares.[46]

Any publicly visible behavioral choices made by the manager can affect stock prices, including dividend announcements as well as decisions to borrow or issue new equity. Another important source of information periodically released by the firm is its accounting statement. There is plenty of evidence that stock prices respond to reported profits in a firm's accounting report, giving the manager an incentive to care about this number.

Accounting profits differ from taxable profits in a number of ways, giving the firm some discretion to change one without changing the other. But the tax law in the United States requires that the accounting rule for inventories that the firm chooses for accounting purposes must be used as well for tax purposes. The basic choice the firm has is between FIFO (first-in-first-out) and LIFO (last-in-first-out).

When the firm uses a good in production that had been in inventory, it is required to deduct the cost of this good from both its taxable and its accounting profits. Among the goods still in inventory, the price paid will vary, largely depending on when they were purchased. Since the inflation rate is almost always positive, the price paid for recently purchased items will normally be higher than the price paid for the same item in earlier periods. As a result, reported profits would be lower with LIFO than with FIFO.

There is a parallel effect of the firm's choice of inventory accounting rule on its balance sheet, listing assets and liabilities. The value of the firm's goods in inventory depends on the prices paid for these goods, based on the chosen accounting rule. Under FIFO accounting, the goods purchased most recently

---

[46] The same incentive to have a high share price in the future exists if the manager owns options on the firm's shares that can be exercised in the near future.

remain in inventory, whereas, under LIFO accounting, the goods remaining in inventory could have been purchased far in the past and have a much lower value. Book assets are therefore higher when using FIFO.

For tax purposes, the firm then gains from use of LIFO, because its taxable income is smaller. But, for accounting purposes, it loses because the price the manager receives on any stock sold will likely be lower due to the lower reported profits and the less favorable balance sheet figures.[47] Even during periods of substantial inflation, where the choice to use LIFO would be particularly advantageous for tax purposes, most firms choose FIFO. They are willing to pay a real price, through higher tax obligations, in order to report higher accounting profits.

A similar observation was made using Swedish data by Kannianen and Södersten (1995). In Sweden, as in the United States, firms have a choice among various depreciation schedules, including both straight-line depreciation and various more accelerated formulas. For tax purposes, the firm normally gains from choosing the most accelerated formula, in order to save on taxes sooner rather than later. In Sweden, unlike the United States, though, the depreciation formula chosen for tax purposes must also be used for accounting purposes. While most firms in the United States choose the most accelerated depreciation formula for tax purposes, as would be expected, firms in Sweden typically choose the slowest depreciation schedule (straight-line), yielding higher accounting profits even at the expense of higher tax payments.

Note that this concern with accounting profits exists mainly for publicly traded firms. For closely held firms, any trades of shares are likely to be among individuals who are closely affiliated with the firm, whose information goes far beyond what is in the accounting reports. But for publicly traded firms, share prices are set based on the collective views of investors as a whole, for whom accounting reports are a primary source of information.

The same line of reasoning then suggests that publicly traded firms will, if anything, exaggerate their reported profits, even at the expense of having to pay more taxes as a result. A dramatic example of this was revealed when the firm World Com went bankrupt in 2002. World Com manipulated its profits by depreciating goods that should have been expensed, leading to higher accounting profits. It then chose to hide this manipulation by using the same misclassification for tax purposes, leading to a substantial increase in its tax payments.[48] IRS audits certainly show dramatic underreporting of taxable income among closely held firms rather than the overreporting sometimes documented among

---

[47] One question, though, is whether shareholders will correct for this effect of accounting rules on reported profits. Available evidence suggests that the market does not adequately correct for this.

[48] See Erickson et al. (2004) for evidence that this is a common occurrence.

publicly traded firms. Perhaps as a result, some countries have implemented subsidies to firms if they choose to become publicly traded.

If managers care about accounting profits, this can complicate the analysis of many of the decisions we discussed in section 2. For example, use of debt leads to lower reported accounting profits per share, due to the deduction of nominal interest payments. A concern with accounting profits therefore provides a different explanation for why firms choose not to make greater use of tax incentives favoring debt finance.

2.8 Taxes and Business Risk-Taking

To what degree does the tax law differentially affect safer vs. more risky projects?

To examine this, we start with a capital-asset pricing model (CAPM) in which individual h makes choices to maximize a mean-variance utility function: $U_h\left(E\left(\tilde{Y}_h\right), var\left(\tilde{Y}_h\right)\right)$. Consider investments either in a risk-free security with an after-tax return of $r(1 - m_h)$ or in a risky security with a pretax return of [49] $\tilde{e}$ and an after-tax return of $\tilde{e}(1 - g_h)$. If the fraction of the individual's wealth of W_h invested in the risky security is φ_h, then $\tilde{Y} = W_h[\varphi_h\tilde{e}(1 - g_h) + (1 - \varphi_h)r(1 - m_h)] + \tilde{Z}_h + \gamma_h\tilde{T}$, where nonportfolio income is denoted by $\tilde{Z}_h$, while γ_h is the share received by individual h, in cash or in kind, from the expenditures financed by the government's total tax revenue of $\tilde{T}$.

The first-order condition for φ_h equals

$$\bar{e}(1 - g_h) - r(1 - m_h) = \theta_h Cov(\tilde{e}(1 - g_h), \tilde{Y}_h), \tag{7}$$

where $\theta_h = 2U_2\frac{W_h}{U_1}$ is a measure of the individual's coefficient of relative risk-aversion.[50]

If there are no market failures in the market for securities, then equation (7) should hold for all h. Dividing through by θ_h, adding over investors, and then making use of the definition of $\tilde{e}$, we can reexpress the market equilibrium by

$$\overline{f_K} - d - \theta Cov\left(\tilde{f_K}, \tilde{Y}\right) = r\frac{1 - m^*}{(1 - \tau)(1 - g^*)} \tag{7a}$$

Here, $\theta \equiv 1/\sum_h\left(\frac{1}{\theta_h}\right)$, $m^* \equiv \sum_h\left(\frac{m_h}{\theta_h}\right)/\sum_h\left(\frac{1}{\theta_h}\right)$ and $g^* \equiv \sum_h\left(\frac{g_h}{\theta_h}\right)/\sum_h\left(\frac{1}{\theta_h}\right)$ are weighted averages of each of these expressions, weighted by $1/\theta_h$, while $\tilde{Y} = \sum_h\tilde{Y}_h$ measures aggregate income. Intuitively, the left-hand side of equation (7a) measures the certainty-equivalent pretax return on the risky security,

---

[49] The net-of-tax return to the firm, assuming economic depreciation, satisfies $\tilde{e} = (\tilde{f_K} - d)(1 - \tau)$.

[50] Here, U_i denotes the derivative of the utility function with respect to its i'th argument.

while the right-hand side measures the required rate of return on this security, analogous to the user cost of capital seen in equation (5).

Note that taxes do not enter into any of the terms on the left-hand side of equation (7a). In particular, aggregate income adds back in tax revenue, so is the same regardless of the riskiness of the equity security. We therefore find that the tax law is neutral with respect to risk-taking under the assumptions used above: All investments in equilibrium earn the same certainty-equivalent real return for any given investor, regardless of their underlying riskiness.

One key assumption was that the marginal corporate and personal tax rate on equity income are unchanged, regardless of the ex post outcome for $\tilde{e}$. If instead the corporate tax has no (or incomplete) loss offset, then the effective tax rate goes up the higher the chance of this security having tax losses. On net, the tax law would then discourage risk-taking. The same would be true to the extent that the corporate or personal tax schedules are progressive, imposing a higher marginal tax rate the higher the earnings $\tilde{e}$.[51]

Another key assumption is that the equity market works efficiently. Consider, for example, a firm that ends up being closely held, due to lemons problems in the equity market. Now, equation (7) holds with equality only for the individual proprietor of this firm. Based on this individual's first-order condition,

$$\overline{f_K} - d - \theta_h Cov\left(\tilde{f_K}, \tilde{Y}_h\right) = r\frac{1 - m_h}{(1 - \tau)(1 - g_h)} \tag{7b}$$

The tax payments made by individual h, based on the random return $\tilde{f_K}$, are shared with the entire population, with only a trivial fraction returning to individual h. The covariance on the left-hand side of equation (7b) is therefore a declining function of the tax rate. A higher rate discourages investment in equity overall but leads to a shift in equity investment toward riskier projects. The reallocation of risk from individual h through the tax system to the rest of the population is an efficiency gain.

A paper by Hail et al. (2017) provided some empirical support for these potentially positive effects of a higher tax rate on investment in risky securities. Their study focused on the effects of an increase in the capital gains tax rate on the value of shares in risky firms. Ignoring risk, a higher tax rate makes these shares less valuable. But the resulting reallocation of risk can make them more valuable. Their empirical work often finds a positive effect of a higher capital gains tax rate on firm values and particularly for riskier firms in settings

---

[51] Risk-taking could be subsidized though if $m > \tau^*$ since a firm can then choose to be noncorporate when it has losses (to make these losses immediately deductible against other personal income) but to be corporate when it has profits.

with a low value of r (where the term on the right-hand side becomes less important).

2.9 Use of "Sufficient Statistics"

To what degree can we summarize the combined efficiency costs of all of the above behavioral responses to taxes by corporations with some "sufficient statistic"? Following the logic developed in Feldstein (1995) and Chetty (2009), what we would need is some measure of the implications of these behavioral responses for overall government revenue.

In past work on distortions created by the personal income tax, the proposed sufficient statistics focus on the implications of any behavioral responses for taxable personal income year by year. What would be the equivalent when looking at corporate changes in behavior?

The direct analogue with this past literature on the personal income tax would be to estimate changes in corporate tax payments (or in taxable corporate income) due to behavioral responses to a tax reform. This was the focus in Devereux et al. (2014), looking at the response to corporate tax changes in the UK.

The key omitted complication here, and one present as well in the use of sufficient statistics for the efficiency costs of changes in the personal tax code, is the implications of a tax reform for shifting of income between the personal and the corporate tax base. If effective tax rates are equal in the two settings, then there are no added complications. But to the extent that effective tax rates differ, then shifting of income from a high tax rate to a low tax rate results in an added efficiency cost, and conversely.

The timing of income might also be affected by changes in the tax code and matters to the extent that effective tax rates change over time. In addition, international income shifting could respond to changes in the tax code and the impact of this response for the present value of domestic tax revenue also should be part of any sufficient statistic.

3 Optimal Corporate Tax Structure

How *should* the corporate tax base be designed, and how *should* the corporate tax rate compare to the personal tax rate?[52]

We will think through this question in stages. Our first focus will be based on a set of assumptions, laid out in section 3.1, where on normative grounds there is no reason to treat income differently simply depending on whether it was earned

---

[52] Discussion in this section draws heavily from Gordon (2012). For a prior survey of the domestic case, see Mintz (1996).

in the corporate or noncorporate sector and where there are none of the market failures that came up in section 2 when trying to explain observed corporate behavior. In section 3.2, we will then work through the characteristics of the optimal corporate tax under these assumptions, focusing on a closed economy setting. In section 3.3, we then turn to thinking through how to extend these results to an open economy setting with cross-border portfolio investments as well as both inbound and outbound FDI.

3.1 Setup of the Analysis

3.1.1 Initial Assumptions

The underlying aim of our analysis is to solve for the optimal tax structure for a corporate income tax given the optimal personal income tax structure.[53] There have been many studies in the past examining the characteristics, and particularly the rate structure, for an optimal personal income tax. We assume that this analysis of the optimal personal income tax leads to an optimal marginal tax rate on personal income from labor equal to m, with this optimal rate varying by individual, and an optimal marginal tax rate on income from savings equal to am.[54]

The key innovation in this Element is to extend these results to think about the optimal corporate income tax structure.

Our starting point is an assumption that the tax rate on any given source of income should be the same, regardless of the sector where it was earned. One initial justification for this equal treatment of income is the argument by Diamond and Mirrlees (1971) that, in the presence of optimal proportional taxes on factor supplies and consumption bundles, the optimal tax structure should avoid any distortions to how goods are produced. Any such production distortions not only change the relative prices of different factors or different consumer goods, as can also be done using differential factor taxes or differential retail sales tax rates, but, in addition, add extra costs due to the resulting inefficiencies in production. The second-best tax structure should avoid such production inefficiencies.

---

[53] In particular, we ignore for simplicity in this Element the effects of corporate tax provisions on the optimal personal tax structure. To the degree that the corporate tax helps discourage income shifting, though, observed personal income becomes a better proxy for the unobserved ability level of each taxpayer; and behavioral responses becomes smaller and have less impact on tax revenue, leading to a more progressive optimal personal tax structure.

[54] Income from savings may be taxed, for example, if this income serves as an additional proxy for earnings ability, even conditional on observed labor income, as found in Gordon and Kopczuk (2014).

One assumption in the Diamond and Mirrlees (1971) derivation worth noting is that either there is no lump-sum income (often referred to as "rents") or that these rents already face a confiscatory tax, taking full advantage of a nondistorting source of income. These rents could come from existing capital at the time of the tax reform or from entrepreneurial ideas that continue to generate a higher rate of return. Our assumption is that any rents existing at the time of the tax reform in the past were already captured, so that we are looking at the continuing implications of the optimal policy.

Saez (2002) provides a more general set of assumptions supporting production efficiency, in a context with both a nonlinear tax on labor income and equity considerations. He finds no grounds for deviating from production efficiency in our context if the following two conditions are satisfied: (1) the location (corporate vs. noncorporate or US vs. abroad) of an individual's earnings conveys no additional information about their marginal utility of income beyond what is known based on their observed labor income; (2) any tax on some activity affects labor supply simply due to the resulting changes in the individual's real wage rate, regardless of the location where these earnings arise.

3.1.2 Taxation of Noncorporate Businesses

Observed noncorporate business income includes returns to both labor and capital, with a different desired tax rate on each. To tax labor income at the same rate whether the individual is an employee or runs a noncorporate business, noncorporate income net of depreciation deductions needs to be taxed at the same rate as the individual's wage and salary income, m, to avoid any distortions to this occupational choice.

The effective tax rate on capital invested in a noncorporate firm then depends on the chosen tax depreciation provisions. These provisions can be designed to yield any desired effective tax rate on new investment, even given that the resulting income net of depreciation is taxed at rate m. For example, expensing yields a zero effective tax rate on such business investments whereas economic depreciation leads to an effective tax rate equal to rate m.

Distortions to the allocation of savings are then avoided if the effective tax rate on investments in a noncorporate business is the same as the assumed desired effective tax rate on income from savings equal to am:

$$(f_K - d)(1 - am) = r(1 - am), \tag{8}$$

Given this effective tax rate, $f_K = r + d$, implying no distortions to the allocation of savings.

To achieve this outcome under the proposed tax system in which the firm faces a statutory tax rate of m, the present value of depreciation deductions, z, must satisfy

$$f_K = r + d = \left(r(1 - \alpha m) + d\right)\frac{1 - mz}{1 - m} \tag{9}$$

Solving for the value of z that achieves this, and assuming it is implemented with some exponential tax depreciation rate, d_t, we find after simplification that

$$z = \frac{d_t}{d_t + r(1 - \alpha m)} = \frac{d + r(1 - \alpha)}{d + r(1 - \alpha m)} \tag{10}$$

Naturally, the higher is the desired tax rate on capital income, the lower is the desired tax depreciation rate. Note, however, that the desired tax depreciation rate varies with the individual's marginal tax rate, m. With one common depreciation schedule, the chosen rate will trade off having too high a rate for low-bracket investors and too low a rate for high-bracket investors.

In such a setting, how should capital gains from noncorporate activity be taxed? Capital gains can arise for various reasons. For one, whenever the rate of tax depreciation differs from the rate of economic depreciation, the market price and the tax basis for a used asset will differ, generating capital gains (or losses) at realization. To avoid tax incentives to churn, selling capital in order to write-up the basis to the current market value at the cost of paying capital gains taxes, capital gains need to be taxed at a rate equal to $g = mz$.

To see this, assume that the initial price of the asset is a dollar. After k years, the true value of the asset equals e^{-dk}, whereas the book value for tax purposes equals $e^{-d_t k}$. The increase in the present value of tax savings from the write-up of the asset's basis if the asset were sold would then equal $mz\left(e^{-dk} - e^{-d_t k}\right)$. The offsetting cost from capital gains taxes due as a result of the sale equal $g\left(e^{-dk} - e^{-d_t k}\right)$. Taxes overall are unaffected by this change in ownership if $g = mz$.[55]

Capital gains and losses can also arise due to new information, e.g. learning that an entrepreneurial venture was successful. To avoid distortions to the decision whether or not to sell the firm, what capital gains tax rate is appropriate? If the entrepreneur keeps the business, assume she earns the wage she could get elsewhere in period t plus some above-normal return R, where this

---

[55] Under US tax law, the transfer of ownership could have taken a taxable or a tax-free form. The text describes the tax treatment of a taxable sale. Under an untaxable sale, typically a purchase of assets paid for with stock in the acquiring firm rather than with cash, there is no write-up of basis and no capital gains taxes due. The neutrality result $g = mz$ implies no tax distortion to the choice of a taxable or a tax-free acquisition of these assets.

above-normal return decays over time at some exponential rate d_R. If the original entrepreneur keeps the firm, then the present value of these above-normal after-tax returns to the entrepreneur, denoted by V_e, equals $V_e = \frac{R(1-m)}{r(1-am)+d_R}$. If instead the original entrepreneur sells the firm, she receives $(1-g)V$ for the firm, where V denotes the market-clearing price for this asset in the financial market.

If taxes are to avoid distorting the allocation of this asset, then two conditions must be satisfied. First, the value of the firm in the financial market must satisfy $\frac{R}{V} = r + d_R$, so that taxes do not distort the investment choices of a potential buyer of this asset. To achieve this outcome, as seen in section 3.1.2, the present value of depreciation/amortization deductions must satisfy equation (10). Second, the original entrepreneur's decision whether or not to sell the firm is undistorted by taxes if $V_e = (1-g)V$. Substituting for both valuations, we find that this condition is satisfied if $g = m((d_R + r(1-\alpha))/(r(1-am)+d_R))$. The term in parentheses is again the value of z implied by equation (10). With this value for z, and with $g = mz$ at this value for z, allocation decisions are undistorted.

Since z varies depending on the depreciation rate of a particular asset, g should vary depending on the depreciation rate of the asset as well. If there is only one value for g, then capital gains on rapidly depreciating assets are too lightly taxed, and conversely. The compromise value for g, though, certainly satisfies $g < m$.

3.2 Implications for the Corporate Tax Law: Closed Economy Case

Given this tax treatment of noncorporate businesses in a closed economy, how should corporate income be taxed to avoid introducing distortions to the form of business activity?

What if the above firm incorporates? We have denoted the effective personal tax rate on a corporation's net-of-corporate tax income by g.

Given that $g < m$, corporate shares are treated more favorably under the personal income tax than are noncorporate shares. If there were no corporate tax, having $g < m$ encourages entrepreneurs to incorporate their firm and then retain earnings rather than paying them out in a form taxed at rate m, e.g. wages.

A corporate tax can serve to minimize these avoidance opportunities. To do so, the corporate tax should be designed so that the effective combined corporate and personal taxes are the same as the taxes due had the firm been noncorporate. This corporate tax should be applied to corporate income net of all payouts from the firm that are already fully taxable under the personal tax (e.g. wages, rents, royalties, and interest payments) or fully taxable to other firms (e.g. payments for inputs).[56]

Tax distortions to the form of organization (and the resulting production inefficiencies) can then be avoided if $\tau^* = m$ and if the depreciation rate for corporate investments satisfies equation (10).[57] Given these tax provisions, all returns to labor effort (entrepreneurial income) are taxed at an effective tax rate m and all income from savings is taxed at rate am, regardless of the organizational form of the firm.

Note that the optimal corporate rate depends on the characteristics of the personal tax system. If capital gains are tax exempt, then the corporate tax rate should simply equal m, whereas if capital gains are taxable in full at accrual, with $g = m$, then the optimum has $\tau = 0$.

Note, though, that $\tau^* = m$ for only one value of $(1 - m)/(1 - g)$. In the presence of a progressive personal income tax schedule, the choice of a corporate tax schedule must trade off cases where the resulting distortions go in different directions. Individuals with $m > \tau^*$ can save on taxes by shifting their income into the corporate sector, while those with $m < \tau^*$ face a tax penalty from accruing corporate income.[58]

The optimal compromise rate would be below the top personal tax rate but likely not by much since most of the income-shifting opportunities are available to individuals in the top personal tax brackets.[59]

What if, rather than having one corporate tax rate, instead the government can choose a flexible schedule of corporate tax rates as a function of each corporation's income? For firms with any given level of corporate income, distortions depend on the corporate tax rate for these firms compared with the personal tax rates among workers and investors in these firms. If firms with lower corporate income also tend to have workers and investors facing lower values of m, then there would be a case for a progressive corporate tax schedule.

As seen in section 2, the distortions, due to variation in both m and τ are at the heart of several parallel literatures dealing with corporate decisions. For one, these rate differences are the focus in discussions of the choice between corporate and noncorporate forms of business. They are central to discussions

---

[56] In the United States, in the past, dividends were also fully taxable under the personal tax, so that the same logic would say they should be deductible under the corporate tax base. That one or another market failure seems needed to explain the payout of dividends complicates the application of this logic to dividends.

[57] Note that any further base broadening (a reduction in the corporate tax rate below m offset by a reduction in the depreciation rate to preserve investment incentives) introduces productive inefficiencies.

[58] See Feldstein and Slemrod (1980) for an early recognition of these distortions.

[59] For example, Gordon and Slemrod (2000) find that reported corporate income responds much more to the top personal tax rates than to tax rates in lower brackets.

of taxes and use of debt vs. equity finance. They also enter into discussions of forms of compensation, given that employees can convert wage income into capital gains through becoming self-employed or receiving compensation in the form of underpriced corporate equity.

Not all countries with a corporate tax, though, have a personal tax, or at least one covering a sizeable fraction of the population. The key issue now is the corporate tax base, rather than the tax rate. Any corporate expenditures that are deductible and not taxed elsewhere (e.g. not payments to other corporations taxable there) avoid tax entirely, opening up an incentive to convert nondeductible forms of expenditures into forms that are deductible. For example, shareholders can buy capital directly and rent it to the firm, with rent payments deductible in full, rather than having the firm buy the capital and face only gradual deductions for depreciation expenses. Similarly, if wage payments are fully deductible, then all entrepreneurial income (from both capital and labor) can be paid out as wages and escape corporate tax yet not face any personal taxes.

To avoid opening up these avoidance routes, deductions should be allowed only for purchases from other firms that are taxable there.[60] Note that this is just what is done with a VAT.

3.3 Optimal Design of a Corporate Tax in an Open Economy

Section 3.2, and much of the past literature on the effects of corporate vs. noncorporate tax rates, focuses on purely domestic firms. Yet, with globalization, an increasing fraction of GDP is produced by multinationals, while cross-border portfolio flows are also of increasing importance. How would the above results about the optimal design of the corporate tax be extended to an open economy?[61]

We consider several specific situations in turn: inbound portfolio investment (FPI), outbound FPI, outbound FDI undertaken by domestic multinationals, and inbound FDI. Throughout, we draw on our key assumption that the optimal tax structure should avoid production inefficiencies, so avoid any distortions to how the labor supply or savings of domestic residents are allocated across firms or across locations.

---

[60] Alternatively, schedular taxes (e.g. a payroll tax in the case of wages) could be imposed on each form of deductible payout, at a rate equal to the corporate tax rate.

[61] Here, we maintain the same objective function used above for each country and implicitly solve for the Nash equilibrium policies. This Nash equilibrium will be Pareto optimal when all countries are small. As emphasized in Keen and Wildasin (2004), though, there are other Pareto efficient policies that raise welfare in some countries at the expense of lowering it in other countries.

3.3.1 Taxation of Inbound Portfolio Investment

From a domestic perspective, how should inbound portfolio investment be taxed? If the country is a price taker in the world capital market, then the Diamond and Mirrlees (1971) result implies that the income accruing to foreign portfolio owners should not be taxed.[62] This implies to begin with that this income should not be subject to withholding taxes.[63] However, in addition it implies that the investment should not be subject to domestic corporate income taxes either. Corporate taxation of foreign capital invested in the domestic economy discourages gains from trade in capital, a distortion that should not be part of an optimal tax structure in a small open economy.

To eliminate domestic tax on inbound portfolio investments, one approach is to expense investments undertaken by any domestic firm to the degree that the return accrues to foreign shareholders, and to depreciate investments at the rate implied by equation (10) to the degree that the return accrues to domestic shareholders.

Note that this tax exemption for inbound FPI creates a financial incentive for domestic residents to hide information about their country of residence when investing in domestic shares, e.g. routing their savings through a country that hides the identity of the investor. Regardless, firms do not know the residence of many of their shareholders, since many shareholders own shares indirectly, e.g. through pension funds or indexed funds.

3.3.2 Taxation of Outbound Portfolio Investments

If the domestic corporate tax rate has been chosen so that $\tau^* = m$, then individuals face no tax distortion when they choose whether to be an employee or become an entrepreneur setting up either a noncorporate or a corporate business. Similarly, investors face no tax distortions to the *form* of their savings if equation (10) holds for z: they face a tax rate of am whether they invest their savings in bonds, a noncorporate business, or corporate capital.

What if they invest some of their savings in foreign bonds? Individuals face no domestic tax distortions among alternative bond investments as long as the effective tax rate on the resulting real interest income is the same. Uncovered interest parity implies that the pretax interest rates will differ due to expected changes in the exchange rate between the two currencies. Neutrality would

---

[62] When a country is not a price taker in the international capital market, it can make use of the tax law to take advantage of its market power. Countries, though, would then have an incentive to agree mutually to cut these tax rates through international tax treaties.

[63] Most countries impose a tax called a withholding tax on payments of interest and dividends to foreign investors, nominally in lieu of domestic personal income taxes. These withholding tax rates are often reduced as part of bilateral tax treaties.

therefore require that accruing capital gains or losses on the bond principal be included in taxable income each year.[64]

What about purchases of foreign equity? To avoid distorting the type of equity individuals invest in, the country's effective tax rate must be the same on both foreign and domestic equity. The return to both forms of equity is taxed under the personal tax at rate g. For investments in domestic equity, there is an additional corporate tax on the income from corporate investments sufficient to ensure that the combined corporate plus capital gains tax rate results in an overall tax rate of m. To ensure the same effective tax rate on purchases of foreign equity, a corporate surtax would also need to be imposed at accrual on the return to foreign firms to the extent that their shares are owned by domestic investors.

There are several important obstacles to such policies. For one, these policies imply that any publicly traded firm faces taxation by the government in each country of residence of some of its shareholders. The definition of taxable corporate income in general will vary by country. The result is a substantial administrative burden on any publicly traded firm.

An additional administrative problem is that nonresident governments have no access to the records of local banks and other financial intermediaries needed to audit the tax base of foreign firms whose shares are partly owned by domestic investors.

A third administrative problem is monitoring the foreign investments of domestic residents. Foreign firms are under no legal obligation to report the earnings of their shareholders to any government other than the government in the country in which the firm is located. A (partial) solution to these problems has been bilateral tax treaties. Through such treaties most countries have agreed to some degree of sharing of information about such cross-border income flows.

When firms face different corporate tax rates on the income accruing to investors residing in different countries, to compensate they would be under pressure to vary their dividend payments to reflect these differences in after-tax earnings, depending on the country of residence of that investor. Firms have never faced this pressure in the past, making it hard to forecast how markets would respond to these pressures. Giving firms the discretion to vary their dividend payout rate by country of residence of each shareholder invites exploitation of any differential market power the firm might have in the equity market in various countries.

The dominant problem, though, is that, by international tax conventions, a country is not granted the right to impose a corporate tax on the profits of

---

[64] Any deviations from neutrality open up arbitrage possibilities, with investors going short in bonds with a high taxable interest rate and long in bonds with a low taxable interest rate. See Gordon (1986) for further discussion.

a foreign firm, even if the firm has domestic shareholders, unless the firm is a subsidiary of a multinational based in the home country. Such a restriction is a natural way to avoid arbitrary taxes on economic activity in other countries. However, this restriction prevents countries from imposing neutral taxation on outbound FPI, leading to excess FPI.[65]

3.3.3 Taxation of Outbound FDI

In order to assure uniform taxation of the labor income of domestic residents at rate m and capital income at rate am, the domestic government would want to impose a corporate tax each year at a rate $\tau^* = m$ on the resulting foreign-source income and to allow depreciation deductions leading to the value of z satisfying equation (10) to the extent that the firm has domestic shareholders. With this tax treatment, any entrepreneurial income retained within the foreign subsidiary becomes taxable at the domestic corporate tax rate and then taxable again as capital gains, implying an effective tax rate equal to m.

One complication with such a tax on foreign-source entrepreneurial income based on the residence of the entrepreneur is that the tax creates an incentive on the entrepreneur to change residence. The main issue is tax deferral. Individuals may come up with a very profitable idea but the resulting taxable income shows up gradually over many years. Emigration can then reduce taxes due on all future taxable income generated by past effort and ideas.[66] Akcigit et al. (2016) do detect a small rate of emigration of successful entrepreneurs in response to high tax rates. The emigration rate is small enough though that this threat pales relative to the threat of income shifting.

3.3.4 Taxation of Inbound FDI

To what degree do the above arguments change when the foreign investor in the domestic economy is a foreign multinational rather than a foreign individual?

If a country is small relative to the world capital market, and FDI is just another form of capital flow across countries, then productive efficiency again argues for a zero net tax on the earnings of foreign subsidiaries operating in the domestic economy.[67]

---

[65] See Gordon and Jun (1993) and Desai and Dharmapala (2009) for empirical evidence on the degree to which differential tax rates on FPI and FDI affect the relative importance of these two forms of investment abroad.

[66] In fact, the same situation arises whenever individuals emigrate with large unrealized capital gains on shares they own.

[67] See Keen (2001) for an early recognition for this motivation to provide a preferential treatment of foreign investors.

Foreign multinationals inevitably have at least some domestic shareholders. The optimal tax treatment then would allow depreciation at a rate satisfying equation (10) to the degree the firm has domestic shareholders and allow expensing for the remaining fraction of new investments.

A key complication, however, is that the multinational as a whole may well earn profits above the normal rate of return to capital, due to the value of the entrepreneurial ideas generating demand for the firm's products. These entrepreneurial profits would not show up in the subsidiary's tax base under arm's-length pricing,[68] being fully offset by royalty payments to the parent firm for use of the ideas/technology generating these higher returns.[69]

Nonetheless, the host country may try to impose a tax on these above-normal returns to the foreign subsidiary by restricting deductions for royalty payments or imposing a withholding tax on these payments. In order to assess the incentives faced by the host-country government, consider alternative sources of above-normal returns.[70] One source of above-normal returns could be monopoly profits on the sale of a unique product to domestic customers. Here, the optimal VAT or retail sales tax would be higher, to transfer some of the monopoly profits to the domestic economy. However, there are no grounds for the tax to vary depending on whether the goods are produced in the domestic economy through a foreign subsidiary or instead are imported from abroad.

Another source of above-normal returns could be valuable domestic infrastructure or a valuable legal system, e.g. protection of intellectual property, which together make the subsidiary more profitable than it would be elsewhere. If all firms benefit equally from these aspects of the domestic economy, then domestic land prices and/or domestic wage rates will be bid up to the point that all firms break even, including foreign subsidiaries. However, the benefits may matter more for some firms, e.g. those with important intellectual property, and these firms are more likely to be multinationals.

To the extent that a country is not a price taker in the market for attracting profitable subsidiaries of foreign multinationals, the incidence of any corporate tax on these firms should fall in part on the firms, rather than entirely on land or domestic factors (workers) employed by these firms.

What is the evidence? Two papers by Mathur-Hassett (2006) and Arulampalam et al. (2012) both examine the incidence of the corporate tax

---

[68] An arm's-length price for a transaction within a firm is the price that transaction would have on the open market.

[69] As seen in section 3.3.5.1, neutral taxation by the firm's home country induces the firm to use arm's length pricing as long as there are any real costs of deviating from arm's-length pricing.

[70] See Auerbach and Devereux (2018) for an exploration of the implications of alternative sources of multinational profits on the optimal tax structure.

and find that it is largely shifted to domestic workers through a lower wage rate, consistent with the full shifting of the benefits from domestic infrastructure through higher wage rates to domestic workers.

Given standard errors, though, estimated coefficients cannot rule out a considerable fraction of the burden falling on firms rather than on their workers. In principle, this would make it attractive to impose at least some tax on the profits (plus royalty payments) of foreign subsidiaries operating in the domestic economy.

Even if the government attempted to impose such a tax, however, firms have available many ways to shift profits between countries. Grubert (2003) estimates that foreign subsidiaries in the United States have very low taxable income under US tax law, in part due to royalty payments but also in part due to heavy use of debt finance and presumably in part due to use of transfer pricing. The firm's flexibility in the allocation of its taxable profits across locations implies that there would be little opportunity to gain from the taxation of inbound FDI.

3.3.5 Comparison with Actual Tax Treatment of Cross-Border Activity

The actual tax treatment differs extensively from the optimal tax treatment forecast in sections 3.3.1 to 3.3.4. Under OECD regulations, member countries can make use of either of two alternative tax systems. Under the first, a "territorial" tax system, no domestic corporate taxes are collected on the foreign-source earnings of domestic multinationals. Under the second, "worldwide taxation," domestic multi-nationals can be taxed in full on their foreign-source earnings but with a credit for any corporate or withholding taxes paid abroad up to the domestic taxes due.

Even when free of OECD regulations, actual tax laws differ in a variety of ways from the forecasted tax law. For one, under existing law, inbound FDI is subject in full to domestic corporate taxation, though this becomes moot if the subsidiary reports no taxable income due to income shifting.

Consistent with the above theory, under "worldwide taxation" domestic multinationals would owe domestic corporate taxes on their foreign-source earnings. However, in virtually all countries that used "worldwide taxation," this tax was not assessed at accrual but only when the resulting profits were repatriated. To the extent that there is a tax on the return to savings, this deferral of tax payment lowers the present value of the resulting liabilities. There is no limit to the length of deferral firms can undertake.

Another difference from the tax policies forecasted is the availability of tax credits for any taxes paid abroad, up to the amount of taxes due in the home country.

In the next two subsections, we explore to what degree there are assumptions under which either "worldwide taxation" or a "territorial system" might represent a country's optimal choice.

We show below that the key assumptions under which worldwide taxation, with deferral until repatriation, and the granting of a credit for taxes paid abroad could be optimal are the following: (1) $\alpha = 0$, implying no attempt to tax the return to savings; (2) constant tax rates over time; and (3) no threat from corporate inversions (or full taxation of the return to the entrepreneur in the event of an inversion). Under these assumptions, earnings abroad face combined corporate taxes from home and host governments that are equivalent to having this income taxed as labor income. One deviation from current law even under these assumptions is that firms should receive an immediate deduction when funds are shifted abroad, to compensate for the taxes due when the earnings on these capital investments are repatriated.

A further question is why host countries impose corporate taxes on foreign subsidiaries and why home countries grant a credit for these taxes paid abroad when profits are repatriated. We show below that these added features of past designs of worldwide tax systems make sense when income shifting by employees between their personal tax base and the corporate tax base of a subsidiary operating in the host country is an important consideration. Such income shifting creates pressures on the host country to tax the income of foreign subsidiaries located in the country at a rate equal to the personal tax rate faced by workers in these firms, to forestall such domestic income shifting. Given such taxation in the host country, we find that the optimal tax policy in the home country is to ensure that the combined host-country and home-country tax rate on the income of the subsidiary is the same as applies to the income of domestic firms in the home country: This tax rate is just sufficient to discourage income shifting by domestic multinationals. The resulting optimal tax rate replicates OECD rules, with home-country taxes applying to profits before host-country taxes but with a credit against home-country taxes for those taxes paid in the host country.[71]

At this point, in all major countries foreign-source earnings of home-country multinationals are largely exempt from domestic corporate taxation, receiving a "territorial" tax treatment.[72] The subsequent subsection attempts (unsuccessfully) to find assumptions under which such a policy would be optimal. Instead, it focuses on all of the resulting distortions to economic behavior, which

---

[71] With royalties paid at arms-length pricing and use of expensing, the foreign subsidiary will in theory report no net profits in the host country.

[72] Many countries do impose some supplementary tax on the income of subsidiaries located in countries with a corporate tax rate below some stated figure.

together can seriously undermine the viability of the current design of the income tax.

Given these pressures, section 4 explores alternative definitions of the corporate and/or personal tax bases that help avoid the threats currently undermining use of an income tax.

3.3.5.1 Assumptions Under Which Worldwide Taxation Is Optimal

Assume for the moment that individual investors confine their portfolio investments to firms headquartered in the domestic economy, implying full "home bias." Now, there is no problem with outbound or inbound FPI, since by assumption they do not occur. Any investment in capital located abroad instead occurs through FDI.

Now, the optimal tax arguments imply that profits earned abroad by domestic multinationals should be taxed at accrual under the domestic corporate tax, as would occur under "worldwide taxation," ignoring the possibility of deferral.[73]

Taxing foreign-source income at accrual, though, faces the challenge of auditing the profits reported by the foreign subsidiaries of domestic multinationals. Auditing normally makes use of records from financial intermediaries, providing third-party evidence on the firm's revenue and expenses. However, foreign financial intermediaries are not subject to domestic regulatory provisions that require cooperation with the domestic tax authorities. Bilateral tax treaties in principle could help to overcome these informational problems. But this is not the direction policy has gone.

Instead, countries making use of worldwide taxation have deferred domestic corporate taxation of foreign-source income until these profits are repatriated. The opportunity to defer taxes until repatriation creates a distortion favoring operating abroad and thereby creating a distortion favoring multinationals.

This gain from deferral, though, disappears when savings are not taxed (when $\alpha = 0$).

Assume in particular that the personal income tax avoids any distortion to the return to savings by exempting from personal taxation all forms of income (positive or negative) from financial savings (dividends, interest income, capital gains) and by allowing expensing for all new business investments. Note that, with $\alpha = 0$, investments in capital are no longer taxed, whether they take the form of FPI or FDI: Given expensing for any capital investments, the tax base

---

[73] Note an additional implicit assumption here that this surtax does not affect the country where the firm's headquarters is located. See section 3.3.5.2 for further discussion.

for the corporate tax is profits above the normal rate of return to capital. We can now ignore the degree of home bias, since FPI no longer faces a tax advantage.

Assume furthermore that all tax rates are constant over time.

The key problem faced with such a method for exempting the return to savings is that interest, dividends, and particularly capital gains income potentially include not just a return to savings but also a return to labor, particularly of entrepreneurs who choose not to pay out all of their returns from entrepreneurship as wages.

As a result, there remains a need for a corporate tax for the same reasons faced when $\alpha > 0$. Note though that, with $g = 0$, a neutral treatment requires $\tau = m$.

When $\alpha = 0$, however, the form that this tax takes becomes much more flexible. While it remains appropriate to tax the above-normal profits each year at accrual, it is equivalent in present value simply to tax all repatriated profits. To avoid in the process introducing a net tax on the return to savings invested abroad through such firms, the law should allow an immediate deduction for all funds sent abroad, which compensates in present value for the taxes due on all income generated from these capital investments that are later repatriated. This difference between accrual taxation and taxation at repatriation is equivalent to the difference between taxation each year of wage income and the taxation on receipt of pension benefits.

This taxation of foreign-source income at repatriation corresponds to what happens with "worldwide" taxation of multinationals. Current tax law, though, does not allow an immediate deduction for funds sent abroad, instead exempting from tax the eventual return of capital. This difference matters only to the degree that the earnings of the foreign subsidiary represent a return to invested capital financed with domestic savings, rather than a return to the ideas generating the demand for the multinational's product.

Even if we can rationalize a variant of "worldwide" taxation if countries set $\alpha = 0$, there are two remaining puzzles: First, why do host countries tax foreign subsidiaries at the same rate as applies to domestic firms in the host country? Second, why did OECD rules force countries that used worldwide taxation to grant credits for corporate and withholding taxes collected by host-country governments on the income accruing to home-country firms and home-country residents?[74]

Assume now that all employees can potentially engage in income shifting between the corporate and the personal tax base and not just the entrepreneur. In order to analyze this setting, assume that a firm's domestic production function is $f(K,L)$ while its production function abroad is $f^*(K^*,L^*)$, where both

---

[74] It seems implausible that this OECD regulation would have remained in force for many years if this rule creates significant costs.

production functions have decreasing returns to scale.[75] (Throughout this argument, the superscript "*" refers to values in the foreign country.)

The objective function of the firm is to maximize the firm's overall net-of-tax profits. The foreign subsidiary is assumed to be a price taker in the labor market and must provide each worker with net-of-tax income equal to w_n^*. It can pay workers, though, either through taxable wages, w^*, or through nonwage compensation ω^*, taxable at an effective capital gains tax rate g^*. While wage compensation is taxable to the individual and tax deductible to the firm, we assume that nonwage compensation is not tax deductible.[76] Total compensation must be sufficient to provide workers a net-of-tax wage rate of w_n^*:
$$w^*(1 - m^*) + \omega^*(1 - g^*) = w_n^*.$$

Use of nonwage compensation is assumed to come with a cost $c^*\left(f_L^* - w^*\right)L_s^*$, where $c^*(.)$ is a convex nonnegative function with a minimum value of zero at $w^* = f_L^*$. We assume as well that $w^* \le f_L^*$: nonwage compensation must be nonnegative.

To avoid the equivalent income shifting by the employees of the parent firm, we assume that the domestic government has set τ so that $\tau^* = m$.

The multinational will also charge its subsidiary royalty payments R for use of the firm's technology. Arm's-length pricing would give the parent firm the full return to the technology it developed, leaving the subsidiary with zero net profits (after deducting capital as well as labor expenses). The firm can choose the royalty payment it charges the subsidiary but any deviation from arm's-length pricing is assumed to generate real costs equal to $\sigma(R^* - R)$, where $\sigma(.)$ is a nonnegative convex function with a minimum at zero deviation from arm's-length pricing, when R equals the arm's-length price R^*. The choice for R would be at most the arm's-length price, since any higher R leaves the subsidiary with negative profits.[77]

The after-tax income to the firm then equals

$$(1 - g)$$

$$\times \left[\begin{array}{l} (1 - \tau)[f(K, L) - (r + d)K - wL + R - \sigma(R^* - R)] \\ +(1 - \tau_s)\{(1 - \tau_s^*)[f^*(K^*, L^*) - (r + d)K^* - w^*L^* - c^*\left(f_L^* - w^*\right)L^* - R] - \omega^*L^*\} \end{array} \right]$$

$$(11)$$

---

[75] The contribution of the entrepreneur was to come up with a technology that generates these inframarginal profits.

[76] An example would be equity compensation in a closely held firm. By US statute, workers are taxed on the market value of this compensation and the firm can take this market value as a tax deduction. However, when the firm is closely held, the firm has great discretion in asserting a market value of this compensation for tax purposes. If $\tau < m$, the firm has the incentive to claim that the shares have no value.

[77] We assume here that the host country cannot obstruct these royalty deductions.

Here, profits of the foreign subsidiary are subject to tax by both the host country (τ_s^*) and the home country (τ_s), with the subscript "s" capturing the possibility that the tax rates faced by foreign subsidiaries potentially differ from the corporate tax rate that applies to purely domestic firms in each country. The host country taxes the accruing income, whereas the home country taxes repatriated profits.[78] For convenience, let $\tau_s^e \equiv \tau_s^* + (1 - \tau_s^*)\tau_s$ represent the overall effective tax rate on the profits reported by the foreign subsidiary.

The first-order condition for the firm's choice of royalty payment to charge the subsidiary equals

$$\sigma' = \frac{\tau - \tau_s^e}{1 - \tau} \tag{12}$$

with $R = R^*$ when $\tau_s^e \geq \tau$.

Consider next the firm's optimal choices for taxable compensation w^*. The first-order condition here is

$$c^{*'} = \frac{(1 - \tau_s^*)(1 - g^*) - (1 - m^*)}{(1 - \tau_s^*)(1 - g^*)} \tag{13}$$

Tax distortions to forms of compensation exist to the extent that the tax term is positive. (If the tax term is zero or negative, then all compensation takes the form of wage payments.)

Consider the Nash equilibrium policy choices of each government, taking as given the policy choices of the other government. Our focus is on the choices for τ_s by the domestic government and for τ_s^* by the foreign government.

The domestic government is assumed to choose its tax rates to maximize the sum of the after-tax worldwide profits of domestic multinationals plus tax revenue: Workers and capital owners get the going returns, regardless of these choices. The domestic government is then choosing its tax rates to maximize:

$$f(K,L) - rK - wL - \sigma(R^* - R)$$
$$+ (1 - \tau_s^*)[f^*(K^*, L^*) - rK^* - w^*L^* - c^*(f_L^* - w^*)L^*] - \omega^*L^* + \tau_s^*R \tag{14}$$

Domestic tax rates enter implicitly in this equation through their impact on the value of R chosen by domestic multinationals.

---

[78] Rather than giving the parent firm an immediate deduction for capital invested in the subsidiary and then a full tax on all repatriated earnings from the investment, for convenience in the analysis we allow the opportunity cost of the capital as a deduction each year: Both approaches yield no net tax on the return to capital invested in the subsidiary.

The first-order condition for τ_s is simply

$$\left(\sigma' + \tau_s^*\right)\frac{\partial R}{\partial \tau_s} = 0 \tag{15}$$

Through use of τ_s, the domestic government gains from discouraging domestic multinationals from shifting their profits abroad. Income shifting is eliminated when $\tau_s^e \geq \tau$. At such rates, there is no longer any income shifting from the parent firm, reducing the subsidiary's taxable profits to zero.[79]

What would be the objective of the host country, given this policy choice by the home country? Certainly it gains from extra tax revenue. Since workers in the subsidiary are simply paid their opportunity cost, they break even by working for the subsidiary. Any decreased demand for labor by the subsidiary could in principle cause a fall in the equilibrium w_s^* and/or a fall in L^*. For simplicity, we assume that purely domestic firms have constant returns to scale and are price takers in the international market, so that their labor demand will expand to ensure full employment at the original wage rate faced by domestic firms of $w_n^*/(1 - m^*)$. With an unchanging net wage rate, any changes in labor demand by the subsidiary are simply offset by changes in labor demand by domestic firms. With unchanging factor and output prices for residents in the country, the host-country government is choosing τ_s^* to maximize tax revenue, of which the relevant components are

$$\tau_s^*\left[f^*(K^*, L^*) - rK^* - (w^* + c^*)L^* - R^*\right] + (m^*w^* + g^*\omega^*)L^*$$
$$+ \frac{m^*w_n^*}{1 - m^*}\left(L_T^* - L^*\right), \tag{16}$$

Here, L_T^* is the overall labor force in this country. The first-order condition for τ_s^* takes the general form

$$\Pi^* + A\frac{\partial L^*}{\partial \tau_s^*} + B\frac{\partial w^*}{\partial \tau_s^*} = 0, \tag{17}$$

where Π^* is the corporate tax base. The third term is zero if $\tau_s^* + g^*\left(1 - \tau_s^*\right) = m^*$, since then there is no income shifting by domestic workers: Labor costs as a result are fully deductible and $c^{*'} = \omega^* = 0$. When labor costs are fully deductible, $\Pi^* = 0$. Finally, at these tax rates, $A = 0$ since labor income faces the same tax rate m^* in both sectors. At the optimum, we then infer that $\tau_s^* + g^*\left(1 - \tau_s^*\right) = m^*$.

---

[79] Given the model, the condition $\tau_s^e \geq \tau$ is simply a floor on the optimal tax rate at repatriation. Adding some reason to retain profits within the foreign subsidiary, though, would push for avoiding any tax distortion to this choice.

Given this optimal host-country rate, to achieve $\tau_s^e \geq \tau$, we then infer that the home country will set

$$\tau_s \geq \frac{\tau - \tau_s^*}{1 - \tau_s^*} \tag{18}$$

Remarkably, the tax rate that arises under existing OECD rules governing use of worldwide taxation (just) satisfies this condition. Under worldwide taxation, domestic taxes are imposed on the foreign-source earnings needed to finance observed repatriations. If repatriations equal R, domestic taxes are owed on $R/(1 - \tau_s^*)$. Equation (18) would then be satisfied if a credit is given for the foreign taxes, $\tau_s^* R/(1 - \tau_s^*)$, paid on this income. Under worldwide taxation, the tax rate τ_s on repatriated profits then satisfies equation (18).

3.3.5.2 But the Assumptions Supporting Worldwide Taxation Do Not Hold in the Data

In the discussion in the previous section we made three assumptions:

1) Countries exempt dividends, interest, and capital gains from tax and allow expensing of new investment.
2) Personal and corporate tax rates are constant over time.
3) The country where the headquarters of a multinational locates is unresponsive to taxes.

In the next three subsections, we discussion what pressures arise given that each of these assumptions is violated in the data.

Possible violations of assumptions (1) and (2)

Under the above assumption that $\alpha = 0$, firms would face neutral incentives concerning when to repatriate profits. Either they repatriate a dollar in pre–foreign-tax profits now, and receive $(1 - \tau)$ after domestic taxes (net of credits), or they retain the dollar abroad for a period and receive $(1 - \tau)(1 + \rho)$ in present value, where ρ is the net rate of return to local capital investments. The investment then earns a net rate of return of ρ, regardless of the domestic corporate tax rate.[80]

Yet multinationals are observed to retain large stockpiles of past earnings abroad, as documented for example in Tørsløv et al. (2018). How do we reconcile this observation with the theory?

---

[80] This argument is the same as that used in the "new view" of dividends to argue that a dividend tax does not distort investment decisions.

One explanation for why firms accumulate profits abroad is that the domestic tax law does impose at least some tax on the return to savings invested in the domestic market. A multinational then gains from deferring repatriation of profits accumulated abroad, since these profits can grow free of any domestic taxes when accrued abroad. As a result, income earned by multinationals faces a lower effective tax rate than would be due on other forms of income from savings and the income shifted by entrepreneurs into the corporate tax base faces a lower effective tax rate than other forms of labor income.

A more important explanation for the observed accumulation of profits abroad is likely to be that the tax rate due on repatriated profits is not constant over time. If the domestic corporate tax rate in the following year is uncertain, then the firm has an incentive to wait before repatriating these profits. If it turns out the rate will fall, then the firm gains from having waited, through having its accumulated profits taxed at this lower tax rate. If it turns out the tax rate will go up, then the firm can repatriate before this rise in tax rate is implemented or continue waiting for some year yet further in the future with a yet lower tax rate.[81]

Any fluctuations in a firm's tax rate on repatriated profits then generate tax distortions to the *timing* of repatriations. This opportunity to shift taxable income over time to take advantage of fluctuations in marginal tax rates introduces a tax advantage to investments abroad relative to investments at home (thereby favoring multinationals) and to entrepreneurial activity relative to wage and salary income.[82] For example, the one-year reduction in the corporate tax rate faced on profits repatriated to the United States in 2005 created an ex post reduction in the effective tax rate on income shifted (and then retained) abroad in previous years and increased the ex ante expectation of more such opportunities in the future. The resulting incentive to postpone repatriations in the hopes of additional such holidays in the future creates efficiency costs from this use of a tax at repatriation instead of taxation each year on accruing income abroad.

Violations of assumption (3)

An implicit assumption in the above argument is that a multinational's head-quarters is located in the country where the entrepreneur lives. This is a natural assumption, since the firm would have originated there and since the

---

[81] Deferral can be postponed indefinitely, unlike in the case of accumulated savings in pension plans, where required minimum distribution rules put a floor on payouts. Firms can take full advantage of even rare events of lower domestic corporate tax rates.

[82] For analogous reasons, fluctuations in the domestic personal tax rate favor the corporate form since firms can time the payout to individuals for dates when personal tax rates are low.

entrepreneur gains from having the headquarters nearby. However, it remains feasible for the entrepreneur to relocate the headquarters to another country. While the entrepreneur is still subject to domestic personal taxes on the capital gains on the firm's shares, by shifting the location of the headquarter to a country with a "territorial" tax system, the entrepreneur can avoid any supplementary domestic corporate taxes on the firm's foreign-source income.

For firms with headquarters located elsewhere, only the profits of subsidiaries operating within the domestic economy can be taxed. Profits earned abroad avoid domestic corporate taxes. To the extent that firms can then shift their domestic profits abroad, even domestic profits avoid tax.

This gives firms the incentive to shift the location of their headquarters out of countries using worldwide taxation into countries with a territorial tax system and more so the lower that country's tax rate. Shifting the location of the headquarters is not just a paper transaction, since it affects the legal regime the firm operates under and not simply the location of board meetings. This threat from corporate inversions was an increasingly important challenge to any country that used "worldwide" taxation.

Countries can attempt to discourage such inversions. The gain to the firm from shifting its headquarters is the avoidance of domestic corporate surtaxes on all its earnings abroad, past and future. To neutralize at least part of this incentive to shift the location of a firm's headquarters, the domestic country could require effective repatriation of all the profits accumulated in its foreign operations when an inversion occurs, implying immediate domestic corporate taxation on all past earnings shifted abroad. With this policy, the entrepreneur faces a combined corporate plus capital gains tax rate equivalent to full personal taxation on wage income for all past earnings accumulated abroad. However, the entrepreneur still faces only capital gains taxation on earnings accruing abroad following the shift in the location of the headquarters arising from past innovative activity. To avoid this further tax savings from an inversion, the entrepreneur would need to face corporate tax on the market value of the foreign subsidiary, which would equal the present value of future profits accruing on the entrepreneur's ideas.

3.3.5.3 Assumptions Under Which a Territorial Treatment Can Be Appropriate

Use of a territorial tax treatment of the income of multinationals creates many economic distortions. Since income reported abroad will be free of domestic corporate taxes (even when repatriated), this tax system encourages firms to shift their domestic corporate income into subsidiaries in countries with lower corporate tax rates and particularly into tax havens so as to avoid any corporate taxes on this income. In addition, the personal taxable income of the firm's entrepreneur and employees can be shifted into domestic corporate income and then shifted abroad, avoiding any domestic personal as well as domestic corporate taxes on this income.

Purely domestic corporations, in contrast, continue to face corporate taxation on their income and the employees face personal taxation of their wage income. A territorial tax system then favors firms that operate as multinationals over purely domestic firms. Giving multinationals a leg up in the market reduces competition and discourages new firms from entering, likely weakening innovative activity.

In practice, though worldwide taxation may perform even worse than a territorial system. The experience in the United States with use of worldwide taxation was that effectively no taxes were collected on repatriated profits, as seen in Hines and Hubbard (1990).[83] Nonetheless, the threatened tax on repatriated profits created economic efficiency costs, as firms rearranged their activities so as to avoid taxes on repatriations. De facto, then, a worldwide tax system may be even less efficient than a territorial tax system. It is understandable that countries have shifted away from worldwide taxation as international income shifting has become increasingly attractive.

To the extent there are costs of shifting income abroad, then cutting the domestic corporate tax rate could reduce the extent of such international income shifting. But simultaneously it would increase the amount of domestic income shifting, from the personal tax base to the corporate tax base. A rate cut is on net an efficiency gain if the revenue generated from reduced shifting of profits abroad outweighs the revenue lost from greater domestic income shifting.[84]

Countries do appear to be competing to attract this mobile tax base, in spite of the potential costs through greater domestic income shifting. According to the calculations in Slemrod (2018), the average statutory corporate tax rate of OECD countries fell from 47.2 percent to 24.5 percent between 1986 and 2017. Any fall in the corporate tax rate, by encouraging shifting of income out of the personal tax base, creates pressures to cut personal tax rates as well. There is no reason to think that corporate and personal tax rates have now stabilized, undercutting the future use of personal as well as corporate income taxes as a source of tax revenue.

---

[83] Only minimal corporate taxes were collected as well during tax holidays on the large stock of accumulated foreign profits repatriated under these holidays.

[84] See Gordon and MacKie-Mason (1994) for a formal analysis of this trade-off.

4 Possible Alternatives

What are the alternatives to the current design of the personal and corporate income tax?

One recent proposal in Auerbach et al. (2010) is to shift to a cash-flow corporate tax, under which any funds shifted abroad are tax deductible and any repatriations are fully taxable. The strengths and weaknesses of this proposal are largely the same as those described in section 3.3.5 for "worldwide taxation." The proposal achieves productive efficiency regardless of the location of the firm's headquarters but only as long as (1) $\alpha = 0$ and (2) τ is constant over time. Since the proposal would allow an immediate deduction when funds are shifted abroad, contrary to the practice under worldwide taxation, the incentive to shift funds abroad would be even stronger than under worldwide taxation, suggesting that the pressures that undermined worldwide taxation would exist to at least the same extent with such a cash-flow tax.

Another proposal that has long been debated within the EU is to adopt formula apportionment, under which a firm's worldwide profits are allocating across countries based on some formula, where the formula used among US states depends on the location of the firm's capital, payroll, and/or sales. The key attraction of formula apportionment is that the measure of a firm's worldwide profits should not in theory be vulnerable to income shifting.

Use of a formula to apportion these profits across countries, though, introduces complicated distortions to the location of the factors used in the formula.[85] The firm's incentive is to concentrate the location of these factors in low-tax countries. For example, with a sales factor, a multinational can sell to a wholesaler located in a tax haven, with the wholesaler then handling retail sales throughout the world. It can also sell its patent rights at a high price to subsidiaries in tax havens: The sales price for the patent itself does not affect worldwide profits but helps concentrate the capital factor in tax havens.[86]

Another alternative that intrigues us is a shift away from an income tax base to a consumption tax base under the personal tax. Under a consumption tax base, tax liabilities simply depend on the amount of each individual's consumption and do not depend on whether the underlying production took place at home or abroad or in a corporate vs. a noncorporate firm. There would already be productive efficiency, so no need for a corporate tax.[87]

---

[85] See Gordon and Wilson (1986) for an examination of these distortions, focusing on an allocation based on the location of the firm's capital.

[86] Note that, if the patent remains with the parent firm, its value would be based on its book value, which can dramatically understate its market value due to domestic income shifting.

[87] In fact, introducing a corporate tax would distort production, discouraging corporate activity.

The personal income tax base is already close to a measure of consumption. According to the taxpayer's budget constraint for the year,[88]

$$C_t = L_t + A_{t-1}(1 + r_t) - A_t \tag{19}$$

Here, C_t measures consumption, L_t is labor income, $A_{t-1}(1 + r_t)$ measures household wealth available for consumption (measured as wealth carried over from the prior year plus any earnings generated on those assets), while the final term measures the amount of this household's wealth not consumed and instead carried over into the next year.[89]

To achieve this tax base, all savings would be treated as pension plans, individual retirement accounts (IRAs), and Keoghs in the United States are currently treated, where any new deposits in a savings plan would be tax deductible and any withdrawals fully taxable. Unlike existing plans, though, there would be no penalties for early withdrawals.

Tax avoidance opportunities would arise, though, if some forms of savings are not treated according to the provisions affecting pension plans, as is true, for example, for Roth IRAs in the United States.[90] Given access to Roth IRAs, owners or employees of a closely held firm could receive compensation in the form of equity in the firm with a par value of say a dollar per share, pay tax on this dollar and put the assets in a Roth IRA, and then be able to consume the true value of the asset (minus the dollar) free of tax.

To avoid the need for a corporate tax, *all savings* that are potentially vulnerable to income shifting from labor income to asset income would need to face a pension-type treatment.

The set of assets vulnerable to income shifting certainly includes equity in the firm one works for, which has been the focus of discussion in this Element. Gains from such income shifting can be avoided if securities issued by a firm with which one has connections must be included in registered accounts. Under this tax treatment, the normal rate of return on savings held in the fund is tax exempt in present value, assuming the personal tax rate at withdrawal is the same as the rate applying to deductions for the initial investments in the fund. However, any above-normal return, in particular any return to entrepreneurial

---

[88] Note that this tax base picks up all forms of consumption. In contrast, a VAT in practice includes only around two-thirds (and the retail sales taxes in the United States only around a third) of overall consumption. Under a VAT, tax-exempt forms of consumption are artificially favored, adding a tax distortion that in theory would be avoided using a consumption tax base under the personal tax.

[89] With this definition of an individual's personal tax base, other elements of the personal tax, such as a progressive rate structure and possible special treatment of selected goods (charitable donations, medical costs, or even owner-occupied housing), could be preserved.

[90] Under a Roth IRA, contributions to the plan are not deductible under the personal income tax but accumulations within the plan and payouts from the plan are all exempt from tax.

effort, would be fully taxable, whether this return accrues at home or abroad, and in a corporate or a noncorporate firm. The same would be true when taxing employees who receive equity rather than wage and salary compensation.

Use of registered accounts can be an effective way to deal with other forms of evasion of labor income taxes as well. For example, individuals may devote time to managing their own financial portfolio, where the return to their time takes the form of a higher rate of return on their portfolio. If these financial assets are included in a registered account, then the return to time spent as a financial analyst would face the same tax rate as time spent working in some other job. Similarly, individuals can spend time renovating their owner-occupied house. If the house is included in a registered account, then the return to this time and effort is again taxed at the same rate as applies to other forms of labor income.

Transition issues always complicate any major tax reform. Since a sizeable fraction of savings already resides in registered accounts, the complications are restricted to remaining savings. The transition issue is how to deal with non-pension investments made prior to the tax reform. Under the law at the time of these investments, the cost of the initial investment would be deducted from the sales price when capital gains on the investment are realized. Under the new law, the same could be done for investments made prior to the enactment of the new law but now facing a tax rate on the gains at rate m. Individuals would then have an incentive to sell the shares quickly, since the deduction drops in value with deferral. Better, to avoid this incentive to sell quickly, individuals could be allowed to deduct the book value of their prior investments in the year following enactment or carry over this deduction to the future with interest.

5 Omissions from the Theory

Following Saez (2002), we assumed that an entrepreneur's choice to operate in corporate vs. noncorporate form reveals nothing about that individual's earnings ability beyond what is known based on their resulting earnings. We also implicitly ignored tax evasion either through a firm's understatement of its taxable income or through firms evading tax entirely (becoming informal).

Both of these assumptions merit further discussion.

5.1 Corporate Activity as a Signal of an Individual's Earnings Ability?

Optimal tax models start with the presumption that ideally we would tax individuals based on their unobserved earnings ability and then treat the individual's labor income as a proxy for this unobserved earnings ability: Those with higher earnings on average have higher earnings ability, justifying a higher tax burden on these individuals on equity grounds. Those with higher earnings ability may also save more, even conditional on observed labor income. If so, there would be equity grounds for shifting the tax burden partly onto those with higher savings.

The question relevant for this Element, though, is whether there is any additional information conveyed about an individual's earnings ability, holding total earnings constant, knowing whether the activity the individual pursued was in the corporate or the noncorporate sector. If not, then the tax structure should avoid any distortions to the location of economic activity, the assumption driving the theoretical derivations in section 3.

For example, holding total activity constant, do those with higher earnings ability invest in a riskier financial portfolio, leading them to buy more corporate equity? This might occur since, holding earnings constant, those with higher earnings ability have been working fewer hours, giving them more room to expand their hours to compensate for any capital loss on a given portfolio of corporate equity. There was some limited evidence in support of this association in the empirical work in Gordon and Kopczuk (2014). When equity holdings provide a signal of higher earnings ability, even conditional on observed earnings, there is a case for imposing a higher tax rate on corporate income, setting $\tau^* > m$.

5.2 Evasion of Tax on Business Income

The above discussion ignored the possibility of tax evasion. Evasion can occur through a firm's understatement of its taxable income (the intensive margin). It can also occur through firms hiding their existence itself from the government (the extensive margin), thereby operating in the informal economy.

Consider first the informal sector. Schneider (2005) has used various approaches to try to estimate the size of the informal sector, as a fraction of GDP. His estimates suggest that over a third of the economic activity among developing countries as a whole operates in the informal sector, with some countries (e.g. Thailand and Egypt) estimated to have up to 70 percent of their GDP in the informal sector. Particularly in these extreme cases, any response of the size of the informal sector to tax policy would be a dominant consideration in designing tax policy. Among developed countries, Schneider estimates that around 15 percent of the economy operates in the informal sector, so still an important issue.

Taxes clearly create an incentive for a firm to become informal, to avoid tax liabilities otherwise faced by both the firm and its employees. The challenge to the government is finding these informal firms. One approach, explored in Kleven et al. (2016), is to provide rewards to employees of a firm to reveal information to the tax authorities about the firm's existence and then about its tax base. The larger the number of employees in a firm, the smaller a reward needs to be, as a fraction of the resulting tax revenue, to be sufficient to induce an employee to become a whistle-blower.[91] If this is the main threat the firm faces, then a firm, to succeed at being informal, must hire few enough employees that no employee would be tempted to become a whistle-blower.

Another source of information that could reveal the existence of an informal firm is records from financial intermediaries, a hypothesis explored in Gordon and Li (2009). Tax authorities are typically given legal access to the transactions recorded by financial intermediaries.[92] To avoid detection, an informal firm must then avoid use of the financial sector, operating instead solely in the cash economy.[93]

Dharmapala et al. (2011) explore a third hypothesis focusing on the government's auditing guidelines. Audits are costly, with the costs presumed to grow less than proportionately with firm size. Among firms that might be tempted to be informal, the potential tax revenue resulting from an audit should be closer to proportional to firm size. For small enough firms, an audit becomes too costly to be worthwhile. Given this, even if the government can detect the existence of the firm and its size (with capital stock likely being the most visible attribute), if it would not choose to audit firms below a certain size, then firms below this size can evade taxes without risk and are de facto informal.

Whatever the source, assume for now that firms in the formal sector will not be able to evade taxes. Denote the true (and taxable) profits a firm could earn if it chose to operate in the formal sector by Π, and let the tax rate be denoted by τ, leaving net-of-tax profits of $(1 - \tau)\Pi$. If instead the firm were to operate in the

---

[91] For example, if the whistle-blower faces a loss of L in present value, in part from lost employment but also from social sanctions, but their information allows the government to collect in present value an extra T in taxes from both the firm and its employees, then the reward must equal at least the fraction L/T of the extra tax revenue to be effective. The larger is T, so to first order the larger is the firm, the smaller the fraction of the resulting tax revenue needed to induce whistle-blowing.

[92] For example, the United States now requires credit card companies and PayPal to report to the IRS the total sales receipts above some minimum amount of each firm that accepts credit cards or PayPal. These financial records are also available to public auditors, when compiling the firm's income statement.

[93] Requiring customers to use cash could limit sales. Needing to pay suppliers with cash can raise complications if the suppliers are not located nearby. In addition, firms operating entirely in cash would find it hard to obtain bank loans, since they can provide no bank records documenting the level of their economic activity. Operating in cash would then be harder for more capital-intensive firms, who more likely need outside finance, and for firms whose suppliers (or customers) are not local.

informal sector, assume that its pretax profits fall by δ percent, leaving it with net profits of $(1 - \delta)\Pi$.[94] A firm would then choose to be informal if $\delta < \tau$, and conversely.

The government has some control over δ, e.g. through the size of the reward it provides whistle-blowers or the aggressiveness of its auditing guidelines. When δ is a function of firm size, the government has an incentive to reduce τ in each size category down to the value of δ in that category. As long as τ remains above δ, marginal reductions in τ have no economic effect. But, once τ falls to δ, the tax base jumps as firms shift into the formal sector, generating an efficiency gain.[95] Any further fall in τ creates an efficiency loss, however, as these newly formal firms gain a yet larger advantage relative to the rest of the formal sector. This hypothesis provides one explanation for the progressive corporate tax rate structure seen in some countries.

Each of the above theories, though, presumes that firms in the formal sector will end up reporting their true tax base. But the data hardly support this optimistic assumption of no tax evasion by firms in the formal sector. Evasion at the intensive margin seems to be at least comparable to evasion at the extensive margin. For example, random audits of closely held firms in the United States that were conducted in the past suggested that closely held firms on average understated their taxable income on average by about half.[96]

Just as a back-of-the-envelope calculation, tax revenue in developing countries as a fraction of GDP is roughly a third of that seen in developed countries, even though statutory tax rates are on average roughly comparable. Based on Schneider's figures, tax revenue in developing countries (as a fraction of GDP) should be smaller than that in developed economies due to the larger size of the informal economy in developing countries by the fraction: $\frac{0.35-0.15}{1-0.15}$, or roughly by a quarter.[97] With tax revenue in fact smaller by roughly two-thirds that suggests that evasion by firms in the formal sector (or revenue lost due to corruption) reduces tax revenue relative to what is seen in developed economies by roughly two-fifths.

Of course, firms in developed economies also underreport their tax base, so that this estimate of two-fifths of tax revenue lost due to evasion by firms in the

---

[94] Here, δ measures the costs of keeping the number of employees or the size of its capital stock below some level, or of avoiding use of the financial sector.

[95] At the point where a firm is just willing to shift into the formal sector, it must be indifferent between its two options, so that the shift into the formal sector has no effect on the utility of the firm's manager and workers as a group. However, tax revenue jumps. This jump in tax revenue measures the efficiency gain from reducing τ to δ.

[96] See Slemrod (2007) for information about these past audits.

[97] This formula makes use of the estimate from Schneider that the informal economy is roughly 35 percent of GDP in poorer countries and 15 percent of GDP in richer countries.

formal sector simply measures the extent to which evasion by formal firms is yet higher among firms in developing countries than it is among firms in richer countries.

The question then is explaining why this extent of evasion survives, given available auditing procedures. One common assumption that must be questioned is that tax auditors can detect true taxable income during an audit. If not, then any attempted tax assessment must be based on incomplete information. Let the information available from third parties be denoted by N, let expenses reported by the firm (such as wage payments) that represent taxable income to households be denoted by W, and let the additional information available from an audit be denoted by A.[98]

Denote the cost of an audit by κ. This cost includes the salary of tax auditors, potentially includes the time costs imposed on firms that are audited, and can also include the potential losses from agency costs (corruption) when tax auditors and taxpayers collude at the expense of the government.

The choice faced by the IRS is then to accept the reported taxable income of Π^R (and implied tax payments of $\tau\Pi^R$) or to conduct an audit and expect to collect on net

$$\tau[E((\Pi|N,W,A)|N,W) - \kappa + F\tau E(\max(E(\Pi|N,W,A)$$
$$-\Pi^R,0)|N,W)] \tag{20}$$

Here, F represents the percent surcharge imposed as a penalty for presumed evasion.[99]

For simplicity, we assume that no audit occurs if $\tau\Pi^R$ is above $\tau E(\Pi|N,W) - \kappa$, while otherwise the IRS does conduct an audit.[100]

Given this behavior by the IRS, how should the firm respond? One option has the firm pay $\tau\Pi^R = \tau E(\Pi|N,W) - \kappa$ initially and avoid an audit. If the firm pays less than this in taxes initially, then an audit occurs. Conditional on realizing an audit will be triggered, the firm should pay $\tau\Pi^R = \tau E(\Pi|N,W,A)$ in taxes initially, so as to avoid any supplementary fines, and will then face some additional time (and other) costs from the audit that we denote by d. Paying enough to avoid an audit is then worthwhile as long as $\tau E(\Pi|N,W,A) + d > \tau E(\Pi|N,W) - \kappa$. For simplicity, assume that $d + \kappa$ is

---

[98] For example, information available from third parties could include sales receipts coming from credit card companies, electric and phone bills, the value of the firm's imports and exports, and the value of vehicles registered to the firm, depending on what requirements the government imposes on these third parties. Information potentially available on audit includes bank transactions (both receipts and payments).

[99] Note that an audit does not reveal Π but simply reveals A.

[100] Note that κ can be a sizeable fraction of expected tax payments, implying even low tax payments can avoid audit.

high enough (or the distribution of A is tight enough) that all firms set $\Pi^R = E(\Pi|N, W)) - \kappa$. In equilibrium, no audits then occur, though the threat of audits and potential fines does determine reported taxable income.

How does this tax system affect household behavior more broadly? When individuals choose whether to become an employee, earning $w(1 - m)$ net of tax, or instead to set up a firm and earn $\Pi - \tau E(\Pi|N, W) + \kappa$, effective tax rates are the same under both choices only if $\tau E(\Pi|N, W) - \kappa = mE(\Pi|N, W)$. This can hold only if τ is sufficiently higher than m.

The economic pressures leading to the choice of τ vs. m, though, include not only distortions to the choice of occupation but also any opportunities firms face for income shifting between the tax base of this business and other tax bases (for other firms or for individuals). As one example, any source of revenue not detectable through observation of N can be shifted into these firms, making this revenue tax exempt. Also, higher reported wage payments not only generate higher personal tax payments for workers but also likely generate an inference that the firm is more productive and therefore more profitable. Wage payments then increase both personal taxes and corporate taxes, discouraging reporting such payments.

Note that the firm chooses the figures contained in N, leading to an additional source of excess burden: Tax payments based on $E(\Pi|N, W)$ could easily imply very high implicit tax rates on elements of N. These distortions would not be present when Π is observable, implying greater efficiency costs in taxing business income when only N is observable and therefore a lower optimal tax rate on such firms.

In designing the income tax, there is also a choice between "rules vs. discretion." If the statutes specify a tax on Π, then the IRS is left with substantial discretion to infer the function $\tau E(\Pi|N, W)$, potentially creating uncertainty for taxpayers and threats of holdup or arbitrary assessments. These problems can be avoided through making the use of the information set $\{N, W\}$ explicit in the tax code, e.g. through a presumptive tax where the tax base is a statutory formula using the information set $\{N, W\}$ that approximates $\tau E(\Pi|N, W)$.[101]

Presumptive taxes that are an explicit formula of some more easily observable figure N do exist in many countries. Commonly, the presumptive tax base equals gross sales, where at least credit card sales data could be available from third parties.[102] Given that (profits/sales) $\ll 1$, the firm's marginal tax rate will

---

[101] With this presumptive tax, assessments are based solely on information available from third parties, avoiding any potential auditing costs, possible corruption among tax auditors, and any need to reduce tax payments by κ.

[102] See Best et al. (2015) for evidence on the more effective enforcement of this presumptive tax than of a corporate income tax.

be far below the statutory tax rate faced by firms operating under the regular income tax. As a result, introducing a presumptive tax creates large incentives for income shifting, due to this difference in tax rates between the presumptive tax and the regular income tax.

One way to avoid these distortions with a presumptive tax is to have the tax base for all firms take the form $E(\Pi + W|N)$ and then forego a personal income tax. That personal income taxes play such a minor role in the tax system in poorer countries is consistent with this inference.

6 Optimal Tax Policy Given the Presence of Market Failures

In section 3, we assumed that markets work well, so that the only distortions to the allocation of resources are those created by the tax structure. Yet, in section 2, we found that the corporate behavior forecast in response to existing tax structures under the idealized assumptions commonly used would in many cases differ sharply from those seen in the data. To reconcile theory and data, economists have hypothesized a variety of market failures, including lemons problems in the financial market for both debt and equity, agency problems when shareholders delegate decisions to a corporate manager, and a preoccupation with accounting profits (linked to a concern with short-term share values). Another important concern is inadequate incentives for firms to pursue entrepreneurial projects, given the resulting externalities from such innovative activity affecting both other firms and consumers.

In this section, we will consider in turn how the tax structure might respond to alleviate the misallocations that arise due to these market failures. The gain from correcting these market failures exists even if the tax system has otherwise dealt well with the threats from income shifting.

6.1 Lemons Problems in the Debt Market

With lemons problems in the market for corporate debt, outside investors have limited information about the chance of default by any given firm and unavoidably charge observationally identical firms the same interest rate, even though the actual chances of default (as perceived by the firms' managers) differ. This makes debt finance attractive to firms where the manager knows the chance of default is high and may prevent better firms from borrowing at all and then need to invest simply based on their internal cash flow. There are clear efficiency costs due to the resulting misallocation of capital.

How can tax policy alleviate this misallocation? One possible approach is to change the timing of tax payments without changing the resulting user cost of capital. For example, rather than granting firms a schedule of depreciation deductions over the tax life of the capital with some present value of z, the law could instead give firms an immediate deduction of z when they undertake a new investment.[103] With an unchanged value of z, the investment behavior of unconstrained firms is left unaffected. However, the cash flow for constrained firms goes up by $I(z - d_1)$, where d_1 is the depreciation rate in the initial period, financing at least some additional investment.

Another available instrument is the statutory corporate tax rate τ. Investment incentives depend on the user cost of capital, whereas the firm's cash flow depends on τ. In this setting, the government can cut τ in order to leave constrained firms with more cash, while offsetting this change with a change in z so as to leave the investment incentives unchanged for unconstrained firms.

Note, though, that constrained firms could well have tax losses. This could easily arise with a new entrepreneurial firm that has identified a valuable new product/process. While the firm has great potential, it starts building up a market from scratch, so has little or no initial cash flow and large deductions for its new investment. For firms with tax losses that have exhausted their tax-carryback opportunities, the above modifications to τ leave their cash flow unaffected. In this setting, provisions that relax existing no-loss-offset provisions, such as safe-harbor leasing, would help relax these credit constraints.

6.2 Lemons Problems in the Equity Market

Consider next a setting in which risk-sharing through the equity market faces serious lemons problems, leading many firms to be closely held.

To be concrete, consider a set of firms that from the perspective of outside investors look identical ex ante. Based on the information available to the market, the equilibrium share price will be the same among these firms. The firms' managers, though, have additional information. Managers of firms with high expected returns will find it unattractive to issue new equity, and conversely. If the bond market works well, then investment is not constrained. But risk-bearing is misallocated, with insiders in firms with high expected returns facing high risk-bearing costs.

The question then is how tax policy might be used to improve the allocation of risk without otherwise distorting the economic choices that firms make.

As noted originally by Domar and Musgrave (1944), risk is reallocated from the firm through the government to investors as a whole when τ^* increases.

---

[103] See Jorgenson and Auerbach (1980) for such a proposal.

Investment incentives could be left unchanged through a suitable increase in the present value of depreciation deductions, z.

This reallocation of risk is an efficiency gain in itself. In addition, firms now face lower risk-bearing costs but the same certainty-equivalent user cost of capital, so would increase their investment. With any tax on the return to investment, the resulting increase in expected government revenue captures a further efficiency gain.

We noted before, though, that the corporate tax rate should be set so that $\tau^* = m$. Any increase in the effective tax rate on corporate income together with an increase in z may preserve investment incentives but open up distortions along other dimensions, discouraging incorporation, favoring debt finance, and favoring other forms of income shifting out of the corporate tax base.

6.3 Taxes and Agency Costs

The concern here is that the objectives of managers in a publicly traded firm systematically differ from those of shareholders, even given the best attempt by shareholders to design the compensation scheme faced by the firm's manager. The particular concern explored here is that managers put more weight on extra investment than is the case for the firm's shareholders, perhaps because a larger firm will command a higher level of compensation for the firm's manager. The hypothesized response of shareholders is to limit the "free cash flow" available to the manager to the funds just sufficient to finance the level of investment in the interests of shareholders, with the models then focusing on the use of dividend payouts as the means of controlling free cash flow.

If shareholders can observe the size of the firm's cash flow and have sufficient information to determine their desired level of investment, then they can set the dividend payout rate equal to the difference between the firm's cash flow and the desired level of investment and avoid any efficiency losses from agency problems.

Dividend taxes, though, would discourage use of dividends and lead to excessive investment from the perspective of shareholders. Here, the government can improve allocations by cutting the dividend tax rate while compensating through an adjustment to the corporate tax rate so as to leave the net-of-tax return to corporate activity unchanged.

If shareholders are not well informed about the firm's cash flow, though, then through their control over the dividend payout rate they are limited to setting the *expected* level of investment. Even when expected investment is constrained at the level desired by shareholders, the variability around this mean is costly.

Here, tax policy can be used to reduce this variability. In particular, an increase in the corporate tax rate can be used to reduce the variability of net-of-tax cash flow while adjusting z to maintain investment incentives.

6.4 Tax Response to a Short Horizon of Managers

The financial press often expresses concern that managers are unduly concerned about short-term changes in their firm's share price, rather than focusing on the longer-run prospects for the firm. This short-term focus would be natural to the extent that managers have compensation tied to short-term changes in share prices or plan on selling some of the firm's shares in the near future. Since shareholders have substantial control over the compensation of the manager, and any vesting and trading constraints faced by the manager when contemplating buying or selling the firm's shares, one must presume that the degree to which the manager's incentives are linked to short-term share values has been chosen in the interests of shareholders. There seems no obvious reason why the shareholders' choice would deviate from the overall efficient outcome.

However, shareholders have less control over the regulations affecting the construction of the firm's accounting reports. The Federal Accounting Standards Board, a private organization under the supervision of the Securities and Exchange Commission (SEC), sets rules for these accounting reports. Given the inevitable conflicts of interest among different types of firms when rule changes are considered, and an unclear process for adjudicating these differences, a role for government supervision through the SEC does seem warranted.

There are a variety of approaches that might be taken to judge the quality of the regulations affecting these accounting reports. One objective is to transmit information on each firm's performance as well as seems feasible to shareholders. The quality of this transmission can be judged, for example, by the extent to which share prices respond when new accounting figures are released.

Another way to judge the quality of these reports, though, is their impact on the incentives faced by firm managers, given that managers care to some extent about short-run changes to share values. These reports distort the manager's incentives to the degree that short-term changes in accounting profits provide a misleading measure of the longer-run effects of some economic decision. As an example, any new investment will increase profits only gradually, particularly given short-run adjustment costs in putting the capital in place and training workers to use it effectively. However, tax depreciation figures are normally front-loaded, given available accelerated depreciation schedules. If the same depreciation schedules were used for accounting purposes, then new investments would reduce accounting profits in the short term, even if they will be very valuable over the longer term. Better to adopt depreciation schedules for accounting purposes that match the timing of the return of the associated investment. The current use of straight-line depreciation for accounting purposes certainly does a better job from this perspective than accelerated depreciation formulas.

As another example, when employees are paid with options, for tax purposes there are no corporate deductions until the year the option is exercised. In that year, the firm gets a deduction equal to the difference between the underlying market value of those shares acquired when the option is exercised and the amount the employee paid to acquire those shares (the strike price). If the same were done for accounting reports, then payroll expenses fall in the short term when compensation shifts from wages to options, making the firm appear to be more profitable. To avoid misleading shareholders in this way, what can be (and is) done is to assign the Black-Scholes value of the option as a business expense in the year the option is issued.

6.5 Taxes and Entrepreneurial Activity

The concern that there is too little entrepreneurial activity is long-standing. The presumption is that innovative activity generates a variety of positive externalities, due to informational spillovers to other firms and increases in consumer surplus generated by new products. To what degree can tax policy be used to internalize these externalities?[104] The aim would be to induce existing entrepreneurs to pursue more innovative projects and to induce more individuals to become entrepreneurs.

The challenge faced in designing tax policies that target entrepreneurial firms is to identify which firms are generating externalities and to what extent. Any policy that affects firms using existing technologies to that extent induces a misallocation of resources.

One observable aspect of a firm that many countries target is expenditures on R&D. The challenge here is defining R&D. Many forms of expenditures made to develop a new product/process and to learn how to produce this product efficiently may not qualify.[105] Akcigit et al. (2017) focus on how best to design subsidies to R&D expenditures, given that the observed expenditures may be a very incomplete measure of the overall costs of innovative activity. The key

---

[104] This section draws heavily from Gordon and Sarada (2018).

[105] For example, in the United States any expenditures that occur after the product is first sold do not qualify, even though there may be extensive further experimentation and refinement that occur after a prototype is first used in production. Improvements in managerial practices or in the organization of production would also not qualify.

issue in their paper is the correlation between what is observed (R&D) and expenditures on innovative activity that are not observed.

Given that the definition of R&D inevitably omits many expenditures on innovative activity, are there other tools available to improve the targeting of subsidies on innovative activity? The question is what observable aspects of a firm's behavior other than R&D expenditures might be associated with innovative activity. Gordon and Sarada (2018) focus on two possibilities. First, innovative activity involves an initial period of experimentation trying to develop a working prototype, followed by attempts to design a manufacturing process and a marketing plan to sell this new product. Inevitably, this means a period of losses until the new product has successfully been designed, manufactured, and marketed. Most firms using existing technologies, in contrast, should become profitable very quickly. One approach to target entrepreneurial firms is to treat tax losses more favorably, particularly those in start-up firms.[106]

Second, innovative activity is inherently risky, since the firm is attempting something that nobody has succeeded in doing before. The riskiness of a firm's activity is not directly observable. High risk leads not only to the possibility of high profits, which many firms using existing technologies also report, but also to the possibility of large losses. The more ambitious is the project, the more variable will be possible outcomes. If firms using existing technology find they have started to generate losses, they should quickly shut down, whereas innovative firms can well continue to search for a way around any immediate problems, even if many such firms do ultimately fail. Large losses can again be a good indicator of entrepreneurial activity. Targeting subsidies on firms that close with large loss carryforwards and/or with a large capital loss could again focus primarily on entrepreneurial firms.

7 Summary

How should a corporate income tax be designed? Our focus has been how to design a tax system so that it maintains productive efficiency, even while taxing the income individuals receive from work (and potentially from savings). For simplicity, we have taken the characteristics of the personal income tax as given and have ignored any market failures, including not only lemons and agency problems but also any market power held either by firms or by countries.

---

[106] For example, section 1244 of the IRS code allows investors in the shares of a small start-up to treat any resulting capital losses as ordinary business losses, saving taxes at the individual's ordinary tax rate without the limitations normally faced on capital losses.

Under the tax law in most countries, income received directly as "wages," "interest," "rents," or "royalties" is fully taxable under the personal tax. Noncorporate earnings have also commonly faced the same tax rate. But the effective personal tax rate on corporate income is much lower. Accruing capital gains benefit in particular from deferral of tax until realization of these gains and then benefit further from a reduced statutory tax rate and perhaps exemption through a write-up of basis at death. With no attempt to correct for this differential treatment of capital gains, individuals would have an incentive to convert any income that would be subject to ordinary tax rates into accruing capital gains. Tax lawyers have identified many ways of doing this. For example, closely held firms can pay workers through shares in their firm. The "market value" of these shares by statute is fully taxable income to the worker. But when there is no market price for these shares, as is the case for a closely held firm, then the firm can assign whatever value it chooses to these shares and generally assigns a minimal par value of a dollar per share. Virtually all compensation then becomes taxable as capital gains when these shares are ultimately sold.

The role of the corporate tax is then to provide a supplementary layer of tax on corporate profits not paid out in a form fully taxable under the personal income tax. The rate should be set so that in combination with the personal taxes ultimately owed on corporate earnings the overall tax rate on this corporate income is equivalent to the tax rate faced on wages, interest, and other forms of income.

The above argument though is made in the context of a closed economy. Productive efficiency is maintained in an open economy only if the overall tax rate on the firm's income is the same regardless of where in the world this income is reported. Productive efficiency would then require domestic corporate taxation of the firm's worldwide income at accrual.

Until recently, at least a few countries (including Japan, the United States, and the UK) did impose domestic corporate taxation on foreign-source income of domestic multinationals but only when these profits were repatriated rather than at accrual. The deferral of domestic taxes on these profits provided a more favorable tax treatment than would be available on domestic profits as long as there are any domestic taxes on the return to savings or if there is a possibility of a drop in the corporate tax rate in the future. Not surprisingly, the result was a large build-up of profits held abroad. This opportunity to reduce the present value of taxes through deferral creates distortions favoring multinationals relative to purely domestic firms.

Understandably, given costly distortions to behavior but little or no apparent revenue from these attempts at worldwide taxation, each of the major countries with worldwide taxation has now shifted to exempting from domestic corporate taxes the foreign-source income of multinationals.

The result, though, is a setting where firms face a potentially different tax rate in each country where they have a subsidiary. Their incentive is then to shift their profits into the country with the lowest statutory tax rate, though offsetting real costs can leave at least some taxable income in other countries.

Countries then need to compete for this corporate tax base, leading average statutory corporate tax rates to fall by roughly half since 1980 as markets have become more open. This reduction in corporate tax rates has then opened up opportunities to save taxes through shifting income out of the personal tax base into the corporate tax base. The result is pressure to reduce personal tax rates, to lessen this tax distortion favoring domestic income shifting. Income taxation is being quickly undermined as a source of tax revenue.

What are the alternatives? An option that intrigues us is a shift from the current tax base under the personal tax to consumption as a tax base. Based on an individual (or family's) budget constraint, consumption equals labor income minus funds added to savings (or plus funds withdrawn from savings). Most forms of savings, in the US case savings through pensions, IRAs, and Keoghs, already have this tax treatment, whereby funds contributed to these plans are tax deductible and withdrawals are fully taxable. Key then would be to extend this tax treatment to all other forms of savings. Even if this shift were limited to shares in corporations where the individual has some personal connection, opportunities for tax avoidance through shifting income into the corporate sector would largely be closed off. With such a tax reform, there would already be productive efficiency, so no role for a corporate tax.

Regardless, the forecast is a declining role for the corporate income tax, as we are already seeing in the data. Falling corporate tax rates are now undermining use of the personal income tax as well. Some major shift in tax structures will be needed, perhaps through a shift to consumption as the tax base under a personal tax.

Appendix

Dividends as a Signal of Longer-Run Cash Flow

In contrast to the signaling model in the text, assume now that the manager chooses the dividend payout rate each period so as to maximize:

$$U_t = shV_{market} + (1 - s)hV_{true} + (1 - t^*)hD_t - \psi I(D_{t-1} - D_t) \tag{A1}$$

The indicator function $I(X)$ equals zero if $X \leq 0$ but equals one if $X > 0$. The parameter ψ measures the drop in the manager's compensation when the manager fails to maintain the existing dividend payout rate. (This penalty is in addition to any change in the market price of the firm's shares when the payout rate falls.)

In order to maintain stable incentives over time, assume that the manager is issued sh new shares each period and continues to hold a stock of h shares in the firm.

Assume that cash flow is random, with a constant mean $\overline{F}$ with some random shock $\widetilde{\varepsilon}_t$ to cash flow each period, independent across time. Now,

$$\frac{\partial V_{true}}{\partial D} = -1 - C(\overline{F} - D_t + \widetilde{\varepsilon}_t) \tag{A2}$$

Managers then make two choices. First, they choose the normal dividend payout rate and, second, they choose a cutoff value $\widetilde{\varepsilon}_t^*$ such that they cut or suspend the dividend during periods when $\widetilde{\varepsilon}_t < \widetilde{\varepsilon}_t^*$. The probability of a cut/suspension then equals $\Phi(\widetilde{\varepsilon}_t^*)$, where $\Phi(.)$ is the cumulative distribution function for $\widetilde{\varepsilon}_t$.

During a period when the dividend is cut, the choice of the dividend payout rate that period will be based on the initial signaling model. In the next period, assuming $\overline{F}$ is unchanged, the dividend will return to the value it had prior to this one period suspension.

Note that $\widetilde{\varepsilon}_t^*$ and so the probability of a dividend suspension will be an increasing function of the dividend payout rate. The higher is $\overline{F}$, the higher will be the optimal payout rate, D. Outside investors then infer $\overline{F}$ from the observed payout rate and set the market value of shares accordingly.

References

Adler, Michael, and Bernard Dumas. 1983. "International Portfolio Choice and Corporation Finance: A Synthesis," *Journal of Finance* 38, 925–984.

Akcigit, Ufuk, Salomé Baslandze, and Stefanie Stantcheva. 2016. "Taxation and the International Mobility of Inventors," *American Economic Review* 106, 2930–2981.

Akcigit, Ufuk, Douglas Hanley, and Stefanie Stantcheva. 2017. "Optimal Taxation and R&D Policies," NBER Working Paper No. 22908.

Altshuler, Rosanne, and Alan Auerbach. 1990. "The Significance of Tax Law Asymmetries: An Empirical Investigation," *Quarterly Journal of Economics* 105, 61–86.

Arulampalam, Wiji, Giorgia Maffini, and Michael P. Devereux. 2012. "The Direct Incidence of Corporate Income Tax on Wages," *European Economic Review* 56, 1038–1054.

Auerbach, Alan. 1979. "Wealth Maximization and the Cost of Capital," *Quarterly Journal of Economics* 93, 433–446.

Auerbach, Alan. 1981. "Inflation and the Tax Treatment of Firm Behavior," *American Economic Review* 71, 419–423.

Auerbach, Alan, and Michael Devereux. 2018. "Cash-Flow Taxes in an International Setting," *American Economic Journal: Economic Policy* 10, 69–94.

Auerbach, Alan J., Michael Devereux, and Helen Simpson. 2010. "Taxing Corporate Income". In *Dimensions of Tax Design: The Mirrlees Review*, edited by Stuart Adams, Tim Besley, Richard Blundell, Stephen Bond, Robert Chote, Malcolm Gammie et al. London: Institute for Fiscal Studies, 837–904.

Auerbach, Alan, and Kevin Hassett. 2006. "Dividend Taxes and Firm Valuation: New Evidence," *American Economic Review* 96, 119–123.

Bernheim, B. Douglas. 1991. "Tax Policy and the Dividend Puzzle," *Rand Journal of Economics* 22, 455–476.

Bernheim, B. Douglas, and Adam Wantz. 1995. "A Tax-Based Test of the Dividend Signaling Hypothesis," *American Economic Review* 85, 532–551.

Best, Michael, Anne Brockmeyer, Henrik Jacobsen Kleven, Johannes Spinnewijn, and Mazhar Waseem. 2015. "Production vs. Revenue Efficiency with Limited Tax Capacity: Theory and Evidence from Pakistan," *Journal of Political Economy* 123, 1311–1355.

Black, Fischer. 1976. "The Dividend Puzzle," *Journal of Portfolio Management* 2, 5–8.

Boadway, Robin, Neil Bruce, and Jack Mintz. 1984. "Taxation, Inflation, and the Effective Marginal Tax Rate on Capital in Canada," *Canadian Journal of Economics* 17, 62–79.

Bradford, David. 1981. "The Incidence and Allocation Effects of a Tax on Corporate Distributions," *Journal of Public Economics* 15, 1–22.

Chetty, Raj. 2009. "Sufficient Statistics for Welfare Analysis: A Bridge Between Structural and Reduced-Form Methods," *Annual Review of Economics* 1, 451–488.

Chetty, Raj, and Emmanuel Saez. 2006. "The Effects of the 2003 Dividend Tax Cut on Corporate Behavior: Interpreting the Evidence," *American Economic Review* 96, 124–129.

Chetty, Raj, and Emmanuel Saez. 2010. "Dividend and Corporate Taxation in an Agency Model of the Firm," *American Economic Journal: Economic Policy* 2, 1–31.

Cummins, Jason, Kevin Hassett, and R. Glenn Hubbard. 1994. "A Reconsideration of Investment Behavior Using Tax Reforms as Natural Experiments," *Brookings Papers on Economic Activity* 2, 1–59.

Desai, Mihir, and Dhammika Dharmapala. 2009. "Taxes, Institutions and Foreign Diversification Opportunities," *Journal of Public Economics* 93, 703–714.

Devereux, Michael, Li Liu, and Simon Loretz. 2014. "The Elasticity of Corporate Taxable Income: New Evidence from UK Tax Records," *American Economic Journal: Economic Policy* 6, 19–53.

Dharmapala, Dhammika. 2016. "The Economics of Corporate and Business Tax Reform," Coase-Sandor Working Paper Series in Law and Economics, No. 757.

Dharmapala, Dhammika, Joel Slemrod, and John Wilson. 2011. "Tax Policy and the Missing Middle: Optimal Tax Remittance and Firm-Level Administrative Costs," *Journal of Public Economics* 95, 1036–1047.

Diamond, Peter. 1967. "The Role of the Stock Market in a General Equilibrium Model with Technological Uncertainty," *American Economic Review* 57, 759–776.

Diamond, Peter, and James Mirrlees. 1971. "Optimal Taxation and Public Production I: Production Efficiency," *American Economic Review* 61, 8–27.

Domar, Evsey, and Richard Musgrave. 1944. "Proportional Income Taxation and Risk-Taking," *Quarterly Journal of Economics* 58, 388–422.

Erickson, Merle, Michelle Hanlon, and Edward Maydew. 2004. "How Much Will Firms Pay for Earnings That Do Not Exist? Evidence of Taxes Paid on Allegedly Fraudulent Earnings," *The Accounting Review* 79, 387–408.

Fazzari, Steven, R. Glenn Hubbard, and Bruce Petersen. 1988. "Financing Constraints and Corporate Investment," *Brookings Papers on Economic Activity* 1, 141–194.

Feldstein, Martin. 1995. "The Effect of Marginal Tax Rates on Taxable Income: A Panel Study of the 1986 Tax Reform Act," *Journal of Political Economy* 103, 551–572.

Feldstein, Martin, Louis Dicks-Mireaux, and James Poterba. 1983. "The Effective Tax Rate and the Pretax Rate of Return," *Journal of Public Economics* 21, 129–158.

Feldstein, Martin, and Joel Slemrod. 1980. "Personal Taxation, Portfolio Choice, and the Effect of the Corporate Income Tax," *Journal of Political Economy* 88, 854–866.

Goolsbee, Austan. 1998. "Taxes, Organizational Form, and the Deadweight Loss of the Corporate Income Tax," *Journal of Public Economics* 69, 143–152.

Goolsbee, Austan. 2000. "What Happens When You Tax the Rich? Evidence from Executive Compensation," *Journal of Political Economy* 108, 352–378.

Gordon, Roger. 2012. "How Should Income from Multinational be Taxed?". In *The Global Macro Economy and Finance*, edited by F. Allen, M. Aoki, J. P. Fitoussi, N. Kiyotaki, R. Gordon, and J. E. Stiglitz (International Economic Association Series). London: Palgrave Macmillan, 298–312.

Gordon, Roger, and David Bradford. 1980. "Taxation and the Stock Market Valuation of Capital Gains and Dividends: Theory and Empirical Results," *Journal of Public Economics* 14, 109–136.

Gordon, Roger, and Martin Dietz. 2008. "Dividends and Taxes." In *Institutional Foundations of Public Finance: Economic and Legal Perspectives*, edited by Alan Auerbach and Daniel Shaviro. Cambridge, MA: Harvard University Press, 204–224.

Gordon, Roger, and James Hines, Jr. 2002. "International Taxation." In *Handbook of Public Economics*, Vol. 4, edited by Alan Auerbach and Martin Feldstein. Amsterdam: North Holland, 1935–1995.

Gordon, Roger, and Joosung Jun. 1993. "Taxes and the Form of Ownership of Foreign Corporate Equity." In *Studies in International Taxation*, edited by Alberto Giovannini, R. Glenn Hubbard, and Joel Slemrod. Chicago: University of Chicago Press, 13–46.

Gordon, Roger, and Wojciech Kopczuk. 2014. "The Choice of Personal Income Tax Base," *Journal of Public Economics* 118, 97–110.

Gordon, Roger, and Young Lee. 2007. "Interest Rates, Taxes and Corporate Financial Policies," *National Tax Journal* 60, 65–84.

Gordon, Roger, and Wei Li. 2009. "Tax Structures in Developing Countries: Many Puzzles and a Possible Explanation," *Journal of Public Economics* 93, 855–866.

Gordon, Roger, and Jeffrey MacKie-Mason. 1994. "Why is there Corporate Taxation in a Small Open Economy: The Role of Transfer Pricing and Income Shifting." In *The Effects of Taxation on Multinational Corporations*, edited by Martin Feldstein, James Hines, Jr., and R. Glenn Hubbard. Chicago: University of Chicago Press, 67–94.

Gordon, Roger, and Sarada. 2018. "How Should Taxes be Designed to Encourage Entrepreneurship?," *Journal of Public Economics* 166, 1–11.

Gordon, Roger, and Joel Slemrod. 2000. "Are 'Real' Responses to Taxes Simply Income Shifting Between Corporate and Personal Tax Bases?". In *Does Atlas Shrug? The Economic Consequences of Taxing the Rich*, edited by Joel Slemrod. New York: Russell Sage Foundation, 240–280.

Gordon, Roger, and John Wilson. 1986. "An Examination of Multijurisdictional Corporate Income Taxes Under Formula Apportionment," *Econometrica* 54, 1357–1376.

Gorry, Aspen, Kevin Hassett, Glenn Hubbard, and Aparna Mathur. 2017. "The Response of Deferred Executive Compensation to Changes in Tax Rates," *Journal of Public Economics* 151, 28–40.

Graham, John. 2003 "Taxes and Corporate Finance: A Review," *Review of Financial Studies* 16, 1075–1129.

Grubert, Harry. 2003. "Intangible Income, Intercompany Transactions, Income Shifting, and the Choice of Location," *National Tax Journal* 56, 221–242.

Grullon, Gustavo, and Roni Michaely. 2002. "Dividends, Share Repurchases, and the Substitution Hypothesis," *Journal of Finance* 57, 1649–1684.

Hail, Luzi, Stephanie Sikes, and Clare Wang. 2017. "Cross-Country Evidence on the Relation between Capital Gains Taxes, Risk, and Expected Returns," *Journal of Public Economics* 151, 56–73.

Hall, Robert, and Dale Jorgenson. 1967. "Tax Policy and Investment Behavior," *American Economic Review* 57, 391–414.

Harberger, Arnold. 1962. "The Incidence of the Corporation Income Tax," *Journal of Political Economy* 70, 215–240.

Harberger, Arnold. 1982. "The Incidence of Taxes on Income from Capital in an Open Economy: A Review of Current Thinking," HIID Development Discussion Paper No. 139.

Hassett, Kevin, and R. Glenn Hubbard. 1997. "Tax Policy and Investment." In *Fiscal Policy: Lessons from Economic Research*, edited by Alan Auerbach. Cambridge, MA: MIT Press, 339–396.

Hines, James R., Jr., and R. Glenn Hubbard. 1990. "Coming Home to America: Dividend Repatriations by U.S. Multinationals." In *Taxation in the Global Economy*, edited by Assaf Razin and Joel Slemrod. Chicago: University of Chicago Press, 161–208.

Jensen, Michael, and William Meckling. 1976. "Theory of the Firm: Managerial Behavior, Agency Costs and Ownership Structure," *Journal of Financial Economics* 3, 305–360.

Jorgenson, Dale, and Alan Auerbach. 1980. "Inflation-Proof Depreciation of Assets," *Harvard Business Review* 58, 113–118.

Kannianen, Vesa and Jan Södersten. 1995. "The Importance of Reporting Conventions for the Theory of Corporate Taxation," *Journal of Public Economics* 7, 417–430.

Keen, Michael. 2001. "Preferential Regimes Can Make Tax Competition Less Harmful," *National Tax Journal* 54, 757–762.

Keen, Michael, and David Wildasin. 2004. "Pareto-Efficient International Taxation," *American Economic Review* 94, 259–275.

King, Mervyn. 1977. *Public Policy and the Corporation*. London: Chapman and Hall.

King, Mervyn, and Don Fullerton. 1984. *The Taxation of Income from Capital: A Comparative Study of the United States, the United Kingdom, Sweden, and Germany*, Chicago: University of Chicago Press.

Kleven, Henrik, Claus Kreiner, and Emmanuel Saez. 2016. "Why Can Modern Governments Tax So Much? An Agency Model of Firms as Fiscal Intermediaries," *Economica* 83, 219–246.

MacKie-Mason, Jeffrey, and Roger Gordon. 1997. "How Much Do Taxes Discourage Incorporation?," *Journal of Finance* 52, 477–505.

Mathur, Aparna, and Kevin Hassett. 2006. "Taxes and Wages," American Enterprise Institute Working Paper No. 138.

Miller, Merton, and Franco Modigliani. 1963. "Corporate Income Taxes and the Cost of Capital: A Correction," *American Economic Review* 53, 433–443.

Miller, Merton, and Kevin Rock. 1985. "Dividend Policy under Asymmetric Information," *Journal of Finance* 40, 1031–1051.

Mintz, Jack. 1996: "Corporation Tax: A Survey," *Fiscal Studies* 16, 23–68.

Modigliani, Franco, and Merton Miller. 1958. "The Cost of Capital, Corporation Finance and the Theory of Investment," *American Economic Review* 48, 261–297.

Myers, Stewart, and Nicholas Majluf. 1983. "Corporate Financing and Investment Decisions When Firms Have Information That Investors Do Not Have," *Journal of Financial Economics* 13, 187–221.

Saez, Emmanuel. 2002. "The Desirability of Commodity Taxation under Non-Linear Income Taxation and Heterogeneous Tastes," *Journal of Public Economics* 83, 217–30.

Schneider, Friedrich. 2005. "Shadow Economies around the World: What Do We Really Know?," *European Journal of Political Economy* 21, 598–642.

Slemrod, Joel. 2007. "Cheating Ourselves: The Economics of Tax Evasion," *Journal of Economic Perspectives* 21, 25–48.

Slemrod, Joel. 2018. "Is This Tax Reform, or Just Confusion?," *Journal of Economic Perspectives* 32, 73–96.

Tørsløv, Thomas, Ludvig Wier, and Gabriel Zucman. 2018. "The Missing Profits of Nations," NBER Working Paper No. 24701.

White, Michelle. 1983. "Bankruptcy Costs and the New Bankruptcy Code," *Journal of Finance* 38, 477–488.

Acknowledgments

A summary of this Element was presented as the Richard Musgrave Lecture at CESifo. We would like to thank lecture participants as well as Robert Chirinko, Xiaxin Wang, and two referees for valuable feedback, and Benjamin Osswald and Dan Lynch for assistance with data collection.

Cambridge Elements ≡

Public Economics

Robin Boadway
Queen's University
Robin Boadway is Emeritus Professor of Economics at Queen's University. His main research interests are in public economics, welfare economics and fiscal federalism.

Frank A. Cowell
The London School of Economics and Political Science
Frank A. Cowell is Professor of Economics at the London School of Economics. His main research interests are in inequality, mobility and the distribution of income and wealth.

Massimo Florio
University of Milan
Massimo Florio is Professor of Public Economics at the University of Milan. His main interests are in cost-benefit analysis, regional policy, privatization, public enterprise, network industries and the socio-economic impact of research infrastructures.

About the series

The Cambridge Elements of Public Economics provides authoritative and up-to-date reviews of core topics and recent developments in the field. It includes state-of-the-art contributions on all areas in the field. The editors are particularly interested in the new frontiers of quantitative methods in public economics, experimental approaches, behavioral public finance, empirical and theoretical analysis of the quality of government and institutions.

Public Economics

Printed in the United States
By Bookmasters